Managing Project Supply Chains

To my brothers, Dada, Mejda, Chhorda, Nada and Kuida, and the memory of Sonada

Managing Project Supply Chains

RON BASU

GOWER

Published by
Gower Publishing Limited
Wey Court East
Union Road
Farnham
Surrey, GU9 7PT
England

Gower Publishing Company
Suite 420
101 Cherry Street
Burlington
VT 05401-4405
USA

www.gowerpublishing.com

Ron Basu has asserted his moral right under the Copyright, Designs and Patents Act, 1988, to be identified as the author of this work.

British Library Cataloguing in Publication Data
Basu, Ron.
  Managing project supply chains. -- (Advances in project
  management)
  1. Business logistics. 2. Project management.
  I. Title II. Series
  658.5-dc22

  ISBN: 978-1-4094-2515-1 (hbk)
  ISBN: 978-1-4094-2516-8 (ebk)

Library of Congress Cataloging-in-Publication Data
Basu, Ron.
  Managing project supply chains / by Ron Basu.
    p. cm. -- (Advances in project management)
  Includes bibliographical references and index.
  ISBN 978-1-4094-2515-1 (hbk. -- ISBN 978-1-4094-2516-8
  (ebook) 1. Business logistics--Management. 2. Project
  management. I. Title.
  HD38.5.B375 2011
  658.7--dc23

                                                                        2011025337

Printed and bound in Great Britain by the
MPG Books Group, UK

CONTENTS

LIST OF FIGURES

LIST OF TABLES

ABOUT THE AUTHOR

Ron Basu is Director of Performance Excellence Limited and a Visiting Fellow at Henley Business School, England. He is also a Visiting Professor at SKEMA Business School, France. He specialises in Operational Excellence and Supply Chain Management and has research interests in Performance Management and Project Management.

Previously he held senior management roles in blue-chip companies like GSK, GlaxoWellcome and Unilever and led global initiatives and projects in Six Sigma, ERP/MRPII, Supply Chain Re-engineering and Total Productive Maintenance. Prior to this he worked as Management Consultant with A.T. Kearney.

He is the co-author of *Total Manufacturing Solutions*, *Quality Beyond Six Sigma*, *Total Operations Solutions* and *Total Supply Chain Management*, and the author of books with titles *Measuring e-Business Performance*, *Implementing Quality*, *Implementing Six Sigma and Lean* and *FIT SIGMA*. He has authored a number of papers in the Operational Excellence and Performance Management fields. He is a regular presenter of papers at global seminars on e-Business, Six Sigma and Manufacturing and Supply Chain topics.

After graduating in Manufacturing Engineering from UMIST, Manchester, Ron obtained an MSc in Operational Research from Strathclyde University, Glasgow. He has also completed a PhD at Reading University. He is a Fellow of the Institution of Mechanical Engineers, the Institute of Business Consultancy, the Association for Project Management and the Chartered Quality Institute. He is also the winner of APM Project Management Award.

Ron lives with his wife Moira in Gerrards Cross, England, and has two children, Bonnie and Robi.

ACKNOWLEDGEMENTS

I acknowledge the help and support of my colleagues and students at Henley Business School and Essex Business School in England and SKEMA Business School in France.

This publication would not have been possible without the encouragement and support of Darren Dalcher (Middlesex University).

I am grateful to the many contributors to the case examples and diagrams included in the book, with special mentions to Chris Howe (BAA), Chris Davis (Mott MacDonald), Gary Wright and John Mead (Crossrail), Ashley Rees and Vince Grindley (Fluor), Tim Podesta (BP) and Ralph Fales (Bechtel).

Every effort has been made to credit the authors, publishers and websites of material used in this book. I apologise if inadvertently any sources remain unacknowledged and if known I shall be pleased to credit them in the next edition.

My sincere thanks go to the staff of my publishers, especially to Beatrice Beaup and Jonathan Norman for getting this project off the ground.

Finally the project could not have been completed without the encouragement and help of my family, especially my wife Moira and daughter Bonnie.

Ron Basu

GLOSSARY

Activity Network Diagram is a network analysis technique to allow a team to find the most efficient path and realistic schedule of a project by graphically showing the completion time and sequence of each task.

Balanced Scorecard, introduced by R. Kaplan and D. Norton in the early 1990s, is a concept for measuring a company's activities in terms of its vision and strategies, to give managers a comprehensive view of the performance of a business. Typically it comprises simple tables broken into four sections of 'perspectives' which are labelled as 'Financial', 'Customer', 'Internal Business Processes' and 'Learning and Growth'.

Bar Chart, also known as a Gantt chart, indicates scheduling activities. Horizontal bars show the various activities with the length of the bar proportional to the duration of a particular activity.

Benchmarking is rating an organisation's products, processes and performances with other organisations in the same or another business. The objective is to identify the gaps with competitors and the areas for improvement.

Best Practice refers to any organisation that performs as well as or better than the competition in quality, timeliness, flexibility and innovation. Best practice should lead to world-class performance.

Black Belts are experts in Six Sigma methods and tools. Tools include statistical analysis. Black Belts are project leaders for Six Sigma initiatives; they also train other staff members in Six Sigma techniques.

BS 6079 is the British Standards guidelines to project management. It assumes a full project life cycle from inception to closure and is more suitable for large engineering projects.

Capacity Planning specifies the level of resources (e.g. facilities, fleets, equipment, systems hardware and labour force size) that best supports an enterprise's competitive strategy for production.

Carbon Offset is the process of reducing the net carbon emissions of an individual or organisation, either by their own actions or through arrangements with a carbon-offset provider.

CMMI (Capability Maturity Model Integration) is a process improvement approach that provides organisations with the essential elements of effective processes. It was developed by the Software Engineering Institute (SEI) at Carnegie Mellon University in Pittsburgh.

Continuous Improvement is always looking for ways to improve a process or a product, but not necessarily making radical step changes. If the basic idea is sound then building on it will improve quality. In Japan this is known as *Kaizen*.

COPQ (Cost of Poor Quality): The cost of poor quality is made up of costs arising from internal failures, external failures, appraisal, prevention and lost opportunity costs – in other words, all the costs that arise from non-conformance to a standard. Chapter 3 discusses COPQ in some detail.

CPFR (Collaborative Planning Forecasting and Replenishment): Data and process model standards are developed for collaboration between suppliers and an enterprise with proscribed methods for planning (agreement between the trading partners to conduct business in a certain way); forecasting (agreed-to methods, technology and timing for sales, promotions and order forecasting); and replenishment (order generation and order fulfilment).

CRM (Customer Relationship Management) is the development of the database and strategies necessary to have the maximum client relationships in terms of quality, cost, reliability and responsiveness.

CRP (Capacity Requirement Planning) is a computerised technique to predict resource requirements of all available workstations (also see RCCP). RCCP balances workloads at a high level; CRP will then fine tune the workload balance.

CTQs: In Six Sigma CTQs are referred to = Critical to Quality. This simply means the identification of factors that are critical for the achievement of a level of quality. CTQs in project management are also known as the 'iron triangle' of cost, time and quality.

Cycle Time is the elapsed time between two successive operations or the time required to complete an operation.

Demand Forecast: The prediction, projection or estimation of expected demand over a specified future time period.

Distribution Channels: The selling channels supported by an enterprise. These may include retail sales, distribution partner (e.g. wholesale) sales, original equipment manufacturer (OEM) sales, Internet exchange or marketplace sales, and Internet auction or reverse auction sales.

DMAIC is the cycle of Define, Measure, Analyse, Improve and Control (see Chapter 9 for a detailed discussion).

DRP (Distribution Requirements Planning): A process for determining inventory requirements in a multiple plant/warehouse environment. DRP may be used for both distribution and manufacturing. In manufacturing, DRP will work directly with MRP. DRP may also be defined as Distribution Resource Planning, which also includes determining labour, equipment and warehouse space requirements.

Earned Value Management (EVM) or Earned Value Analysis is an analytical method of comparing the actual performance against the planned performance related to both time and cost in a project.

E-business: Electronic-business is more than the transfer of information using information technology. E-business is the complex mix of processes, applications and organisational structures.

EFQM: The European Foundation for Quality Management is derived from the American Malcolm Baldrige Quality award. It is an award for organisations that achieve world-class performance as judged by independent auditors against a checklist. The checklist is detailed and extensive and covers: Leadership, People Management, Policy and Strategy, Partnerships and Resource, Processes, People Satisfaction, Customer Satisfaction., Impact on Society, Business Results.

ERP (Enterprise Resource Planning) is the extension of MRPII systems to the management of complete business functions, including Finance and Human Resources.

FIT SIGMA (also see TQM, Six Sigma and Lean Sigma): FIT SIGMA incorporates all the advantages and tools of TQM, Six Sigma and Lean sigma. The aim is to get an organisation healthy (fit) by using appropriate tools for the size and nature of the business (fitness for purpose) and to sustain a level of fitness. FIT SIGMA is a holistic approach.

Flow Process Chart: A flow process chart sets out the sequence of the flow of a product or a procedure by recording all the activities in a process. The chart can be used to identify steps in the process, value-adding activities and non-value-adding activities.

Forecasting Process: A forecasting process provides a mechanism for soliciting participation from individuals who have knowledge of future events and compiling it into a consistent format to develop a forecast. The forecasting process concentrates on defining how information will be gathered and reconciled into a consistent picture of the future. In cases where a statistical forecast is used the process will also define how much weight should be given to the mathematical models versus input from participants to develop the final consensus forecast.

Gantt Chart: See Bar Chart.

Gateway Review: The Gateway Review process examines programmes and projects at key decision points in their life cycle. It looks ahead to provide assurance that they can progress successfully to the next stage. The process under the governance of the Office of Government Commerce (OGC) is a best practice in UK government projects.

Green Belts are staff trained to be Six Sigma project leaders; they work under the guidance of Black Belts (see Black Belts).

Greening the supply chain refers to buyer companies requiring a certain level of environmental responsibility in core business practices of their suppliers and vendors.

Inventory Management: The process of ensuring the availability of products through inventory administration activities such as demand planning, stock optimisation and monitoring the age of the product.

ISO 9000: To gain ISO 9000 accreditation an organisation has to demonstrate to an accredited auditor that they have a well-documented standard and consistent process in place which achieves a defined level of quality or performance. ISO accreditation will give a customer confidence that the product or service provided will meet certain specified standards of performance and that the product or service will always be consistent with the documented standards.

JIT (Just-in-Time) was initially a manufacturing approach where materials are ordered to arrive just when required in the process, no output or buffer stocks are held and the finished product is delivered direct to the customer. Lean Sigma incorporates the principals of JIT and now relates to the supply chain from supplier and supplier's supplier, through the process to the customer and the customer's customer.

Kanban is the Japanese word for 'card'. The basic Kanban system is to use cards to trigger movements of materials between operations in production so that a customer order flows through the system. Computer systems eliminate the need for cards but the principle is the same. As a job flows through the factory, completion of one stage of production triggers the next so that there is no idle time, or queues, between operations. Any one job can be tracked to determine the stage of production. A Kanban is raised for each customer order. The Kanban system enables production to be in batches of one.

KPIs (Key Performance Indicators) include measurement of performance such as asset utilisation, customer satisfaction, cycle time from order to delivery, inventory turnover, operations costs, productivity and financial results (return on assets and return on investment).

Lean Sigma (also see Just-in-Time, JIT): Lean was initially a manufacturing approach where materials are ordered to arrive just when required in the process, no output or buffer stocks are held and the finished product is delivered direct to the customer. Lean Sigma incorporates the principals of Six Sigma and is related to the supply chain from supplier and supplier's supplier, through the process to the customer and the customer's customer.

Major Projects are substantial in value and complex in composition and involve multiple stakeholders. The project costs in a major project usually exceed £500 million.

Master Production Schedule: The Master Production Schedule (also commonly referred to as the MPS) is effectively the plan that the company has developed for production, staffing, inventory etc. MPS translates a business plan, including forecasted demand, into a production plan using planned orders in a true multilevel optional component scheduling environment. Using an MPS helps avoid shortages, costly expediting, last-minute scheduling and inefficient allocation of resources.

Monte Carlo Technique is a simulation process. It uses random numbers as an approach to model the waiting times and queue lengths and also to examine the overall uncertainty in projects.

MRP (Materials Requirement Planning) is a dependent demand system that calculates materials requirements and production plans to satisfy known and forecast sales orders. MRP helps calculate volume and timing requirements to meet an estimate of future demand. There are three major types of computer-based MRP systems – MRPI, 'closed loop' MRP and MRPII.

MRP (II): Manufacturing Resource Planning is an integrated computer-based procedure for dealing with all of the planning and scheduling activities for manufacturing, and includes procedures for stock re-order, purchasing, inventory records, cost accounting and plant maintenance.

Mudas: 'Muda' is the Japanese for 'waste' or non-value adding. The seven activities that are considered are: excess production, waiting, conveyance, motion, process, inventory and defects (for further detail see Chapter 8).

NEC (New Engineering Contract) is a family of contracts that facilitates the implementation of sound project management principles and practices as well as defining legal relationships. It is suitable for procuring a diverse range of works and services.

Novation is the procedure of transferring the contract of a supplier employed by the Client to another contractor or back to the Client. In practice, this usually applies to a designer in a design and build arrangement and the transfer of surplus stocks.

OEE (Overall Equipment Effectiveness) is the real output of a machine. It is given by the ratio of the good output and the maximum output of the machine for the time it is planned to operate.

PBS (Product Breakdown Structure): In project management the PBS provides an exhaustive, hierarchical tree structure of deliverables that make up the project, arranged in whole–part relationship. This diagrammatic representation of project outputs provides a clear statement of the scope of the project.

PDCA: The Plan-Do-Check-Act cycle was developed by W.E. Deming. It refers to **P**lanning the change and setting standards; **D**oing – making the change happen; **C**hecking that what is happening is what was intended (standards are being met); and **A**cting – taking action to correct back to the standard.

PESTEL (also PESTLE) is an analytical tool for assessing the impact of external contexts on a project or a major operation, and also the impact of a project on its external contexts. There are several possible contexts, including **P**olitical, **E**conomic, **S**ocial, **T**echnical, **E**nvironmental and **L**egal.

PMBOK is the *Project Management Body of Knowledge* published by the Project Management Institute. It is a book which presents a set of standard terminology and guidelines for project management.

PRINCE2 (**PR**ojects **IN** Controlled Environments) is a process-based method for effective project management. It is a de facto standard used extensively by the UK government and is widely recognised and used in the private sector, both in the UK and internationally.

Process Mapping is a tool to represent a process by a diagram containing a series of linked tasks or activities which produce an output.

Programme Management is the process of managing several related projects, often with the intention of improving an organisation's performance. In practice and in its aims it is often closely related to a common corporate objective.

Project: A project is a unique item of work for which there is a financial budget and a defined schedule.

Project Charter: A Project Charter is a working document for defining the terms of reference of each Six Sigma project. The charter can make a successful project by specifying necessary resources and boundaries that will in turn ensure success.

Project Management involves the planning, scheduling, budgeting and control of a project using an integrated team of workers and specialists.

RCCP (Rough Cut Capacity Planning): The RCCP process considers only the critical work centres (bottlenecks, highly utilised resources etc.) and attempts to balance longer-term workloads and demand at high level.

Risk Analysis: A risk in a project is any future event that may affect the outcome of the project. Risk analysis is the systematic process of identifying, analysing and responding to the project risk.

RU/CS (Resource Utilisation and Customer Service) analysis is a simple tool to establish the relative importance of the key parameters of both Resource Utilisation and Customer Service and to identify their conflicts.

S&OP (Sales and Operations Planning) is derived from MRP and includes new product planning, demand planning and supply review to provide weekly and daily manufacturing schedules and financial information. Also see MRPII. S&OP is further explained in Chapter 7.

SCOR: The Supply-Chain Operations Reference model is a process reference model that has been developed and endorsed by the Supply Chain Council as the cross-industry standard diagnostic tool for supply chain management.

SIPOC is a high-level map of a process to view how a company goes about satisfying a particular customer requirement in the overall supply chain. SIPOC stands for supplier, input, process, output and customer.

Six Sigma is quality system which in effect aims for zero defects. Six Sigma in statistical terms means six deviations from the arithmetic mean. This equates to 99.99966 per cent of the total population, or 3.4 defects per million opportunities.

SMED (Single Minute Exchange of Dies): This was developed for the Japanese automobile industry by Shigeo Shingo in the 1980s and involves the reduction of changeover of production by intensive work study to determine in process and out process activities, and then systematically improving the planning, tooling and operations of the changeover process. Shingo believed in looking for simple solutions rather than relying on technology.

Supplier Partnership: In supply chain management customers and suppliers develop such a close and long-term relationship that the two work together as partners sharing both benefits and risks and both parties have an interest in each other's success.

SWOT (Strengths, Weaknesses, Opportunities and Threats) is a tool for analysing an organisation's competitive position in relation to its competitors.

TPM (Total Productive Maintenance) requires factory management to improve asset utilisation by the systematic study and elimination of major obstacles – known as the 'six big losses' – to efficiency. The 'six big losses' in manufacturing are breakdown, set-up and adjustment, minor stoppages, reduced speed, quality defects and start-up and shut down.

TQM (Total Quality Management) is not a system – it is a philosophy embracing the total culture of an organisation. TQM goes far beyond conformance to a standard; it requires a culture where every member of the organisation believes that not a single day should go by without the organisation in some way improving its efficiency and/or improving customer satisfaction.

Value Analysis, very often a practice in purchasing, is the evaluation of the expected performance of a product relative to its price.

Value Chain, also known as Porter's Value Chain. According to Michael Porter the competitive advantage of a company can be assessed only by seeing the company as a total system. This 'total system' comprises both primary and secondary activities.

VMI (Vendor-Managed Inventory): In the VMI process, the vendor assumes responsibility for managing the replenishment of stock. Rather than a customer submitting orders, the vendor will replenish stock as needed. This process is sometimes referred to as supplier-managed inventory (SMI) or co-managed inventory.

VSM (Value Stream Mapping) is a visual illustration of all activities required to bring a product through the main flow, from raw material to the stage of reaching the customer.

WBS (Work Breakdown Structure) is a tool used to define and group a project's discrete work elements in a way that helps organise and define the total work scope of the project. A WBS also provides the necessary framework for detailed cost estimating, organisation structure, task scheduling and execution strategy. It is similar in format to Product Breakdown Structure (PBS).

CHAPTER 1

THE ROLE OF SUPPLY CHAIN AS A VALUE DRIVER

INTRODUCTION

This chapter explains the basic concepts of Supply Chain Management (SCM) and shows that supply chains in some shape or form are required to deliver products and services that either we – or our organisation – need or *think* are needed. For every business transaction there is a supplier and a customer and there are activities, facilities and processes linking that supplier to the customer. In addition, for every task in a project there is a customer and a supplier or a group of suppliers. The management process of balancing these links to deliver best value to the customer at minimum cost and effort for the supplier is supply chain management. Whilst you may be unaware of them, you will experience supply chains everywhere, e.g. in running your home, managing a manufacturing business, in health services, hotels, banks, government, utilities, non-profit organisations, universities, entertainment, retail, professional services and managing a project.

Supply chains vary significantly in complexity and size but their fundamental principles apply to all operations, whether they are large or small, manufacturing or service, private or public sector. Supply chain management is relevant to all businesses and to all operations.

Let us look at some everyday scenarios to see supply chains in operation. When a customer visits a hairdresser she is the customer and the hairdresser is the supplier. The hairdresser will need to ensure the availability of materials (shampoo, conditioner and colouring), facilities and equipment (chairs, driers etc.). In order to provide the service, the hairdresser is involved with purchasing, inventory management and facilities supervision. In order to minimise customer queues there is also a need for demand forecasting, capacity management, scheduling and quality management. In this example of a basic service operation we can identify the key components of supply chain management.

Take another scenario. Consider that you are checking in at Zagreb Airport for a return flight to London. You are unhappy to find that there is a long queue. You have discovered that in addition to normal procedures the central computer is down and a screening machine has been installed to X-ray all types of luggage as an extra security precaution. In this case the supply chain is obviously more complex than the example shown above for the hairdressing service. For you the customer, the initial focal point is the check-in clerk, but there are many supporting links leading to this provision. The airlines have to sell tickets, ensure the availability of aircraft with all the required fittings (including in-flight entertainment systems) in an acceptable condition, provide meals and a have a stock of trained air crew available. Before you got to Zagreb Airport your administration manager will have purchased a ticket from a travel agent, who in turn may have made an electronic booking.

In this case, we can see that there are suppliers and suppliers *of* suppliers. Moreover there exist both customers and customers *of* customers. However the basic functions of forecasting, capacity management, inventory management, scheduling and quality management are present just as they were with the hairdresser, and just as they are for any supply chain.

The message is clear: the key objective of supply chain management is to provide best value to the customer by measuring, planning and managing all the links in the chain.

In a major project the client may engage only the main contractor, who in turn will select the second tier contractors. In succession they will procure a wide range of works, services and materials from the large number of smaller contractors and suppliers which form the Project Supply Chain of sourcing and delivery.

WHAT IS SUPPLY CHAIN MANAGEMENT?

In a typical supply chain, raw materials are procured and items are produced at one or more factories, shipped to warehouses for intermediate storage and then transported to retailers or customers. If you asked people involved in business to define the term 'supply chain' you would get many different answers. Each definition would reflect the nature of the individual's business and the inputs and outputs produced. For some, supply chain is related to purchasing and procurement; to others it involves warehousing, distribution and transportation. For yet others it would be sources of capital and labour. Swink et al. (2010) provide a holistic definition of the supply chain, viz. the entire network of organisations involved in:

- converting raw materials and information into products and services;
- consuming the products and services;
- disposing of the products and services.

They further state that 'this definition treats the supply chain as a product cradle-to-grave concept, including all value-added activities required to plan, source, make and deliver products and services that meet customer needs.' To this we can add the word 'process'. We see the supply chain not as a series of separate operations and organisations but as a complete end-to-end procedure.

Another useful definition is provided by Simchi-Levi et al. (2003, p. 1):

> *Supply chain management is a set of approaches utilized to efficiently integrate suppliers, manufacturers, warehouses and stores, so that merchandise is produced and distributed at the right quantities, to the right locations, and at the right time, in order to minimize system-wide costs while satisfying service level requirements.*

What do these definitions suggest? They propose that supply chain management must consider every organisation and facility involved in making the product, and the costs inherent in doing so. This also implies that the objective is to be cost effective across the whole supply chain, which requires a system wide approach to optimisation.

Supply Chain in Manufacturing

Supply chain management in a manufacturing and supply organisation considers the demand, supply and inventory needs for each item of production. In particular it looks at how inventory flows through the system in order to achieve output to the customer's specification on time and at the least cost. With supply chain management, customer service is increased through the reduction of lead times, and the product is always exactly as specified and is always delivered on time. Costs are reduced through the elimination of any activity that does not add value and through the reduction of inventories of material and associated holding and handling costs.

Activities and measures based on customer requirements are very significant in improving business performance. However, externally driven customer-based measures have to be matched by gauges of what the company can do (feasibility, capacity, know-how and resources) to consistently meet customer expectations. A high standard of customer performance derives from planning, processes and actions integrated across the whole organisation.

Supply chain management focuses on the critical measures of all elements of the supply chain. Externally these measures include the suppliers at one end and the customer at the other end of the supply process. These externals, the supplier and the customer, are matched with the internal requirements of the manufacturing process. The focus is two-fold: to satisfy customer needs and to keep costs down to a minimum.

In reality the elements of supply chain management are not new – we all have been dealing with parts of the supply chain for years (e.g. buying, planning, scheduling, stock control, warehousing, logistics, distribution etc.) without realising the significance of the whole chain concept. Likewise the cost of the various elements of supply and distribution has been long recognised. 'In 50 years between 1870 and 1920 the cost of distributing necessities and luxuries has nearly trebled, while production costs have gone down by one fifth – what we are saving in production we are losing in distribution', observed Ralph Barsodi in 1929.

It is relatively new to view the supply chain as a process, in other words as a single integrated flow across all the functions of a business. Traditionally activities within a supply chain were seen as separate and specialist functions such as purchasing, planning, scheduling, manufacturing and distribution. However with supply chain management, the flow of both materials and information across traditional functional boundaries is seen as a single process. These flows are depicted in a simplified model in Figure 1.1.

In the past, information flow was the domain of the commercial division, while the conversion process of materials flow constituted a manufacturing or technical division task. With an integrated supply chain approach the responsibility for all elements of supply now lies with Operations Management or supply chain management. In many businesses, the integrated approach is being extended to include all suppliers (including 'upstream' 1st, 2nd and 3rd tier suppliers) through the manufacturing process 'downstream' to each level of customers. This includes distributors, wholesalers and retailers through to the end user or consumer. This is known as the 'extended supply chain'.

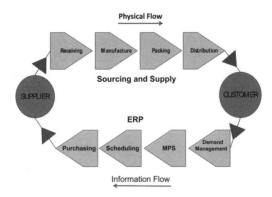

Figure 1.1   Supply chain management model

Supply Chain in Services

Thanks to ease of travel, the media and the World Wide Web customers have never been more informed than they are today. Customers know what they want and are aware of what can be done; they understand the concept of world-class and continuous improvement. This is especially true in service industries. As a result of the heightened expectations of these clients, operations managers in service sectors have been forced to focus their attention on managing the complete value-adding system using the principles of supply chain management.

But just how can service industries apply supply chain management? The supply chain of a service organisation contains suppliers, products or services, customers and their demand for products and service level agreements. Service inventory can be in the form of information databases, stocks of consumables (as with the hairdresser), stationery items (such as brochures and promotional material), and subcontractors (including facility managers, travel agents, caterers and advertising agencies).

Swank (2003) described a successful application of supply chain management and lean production principles in a typical insurance service company in the USA, Jefferson Pilot Financial (JPF). JPF believed that the processing of their almost tangible 'service product' was comparable to a car assembly process. Swank explains that: 'Like an automobile on the assembly line, an insurance policy goes through a series of processes, from initial application to underwriting or risk assessment to policy issuance. With each step value is added to the work in progress – just as a car gets doors or a coat of paint' (p. 124).

Supply Chain in Not-for-profit Organisations

The good practices of supply chain management can be adapted to provide major practical benefit to not-for-profit organisations, such as charities, in meeting their objectives. International disasters have a huge impact on the world's population, increasing the need for aid groups to improve their logistics capability and capacity. Perhaps the biggest impact of supply chain management in not-for-profit organisations is responding to unpredictable demands through quick-response supply and distribution.

The world events of 2005 have suggested that humanitarian organisations are yet to fully exploit supply chain optimisation. For example, referring to the Hurricane Katrina disaster in New Orleans, Waller (2005) was not surprised that Wal-Mart, the world's largest retailer, beat the Federal Emergency Management Agency (FEMA) and the Red Cross to areas devastated by the hurricane. He said the company delivered supplies quickly and efficiently because that is what it does every day. Wal-Mart is the master of supply chain management, and the company's expertise in this area worked well during a natural disaster.

An example of the application of supply chain management in a not-for-profit organisation is the National Health Service in the United Kingdom.

Supply Chain in Projects

The essential success criterion of a project is the timely, accurate to quality and cost-effective delivery of materials, systems and facilities. There are many stakeholders, contractors and suppliers involved in a project. In a major infrastructure scheme such as Heathrow Terminal 5 there are likely to be more than 100 key contractors and consulting firms. Thus, supply chain management methodologies and processes are crucial to ensuring that project resources are delivered as required.

Although supply chain management should be an essential process within the Project Manager's tool kit, its importance in Project Management is not properly recognised. Due to the perception of the 'one-off' and unique nature of a project versus the repetitive nature of operations, the traditional approach of project management has been consciously different from that of operations management. Supply chain management is inextricably linked with operations management (Slack et al. 2006, p. 208). A primary objective of both supply chain management and operations management is to ensure optimum customer service by balancing cost, time and quality (Wild, 2002). However the mindset of project managers appears to exclude the principles and objectives of supply chain management (Ala-Risku and Karkkainen, 2006).

In the context of a major project, supply chain management can be linear or non-linear. A supply chain is considered linear when a material, product or service is sourced from a single supplier. This single-source linear procurement is more common in operations management. However in a project supply chain a major contractor is served by several subcontractors and each subcontractor may be served by several other subcontractors and the process becomes non-linear. Hence the perspective of the linear supply chain includes the procurements that are well defined from a single supplier and perform as specified. On the other hand, non-linear supply chains occur when risks appear from multiple tiers of suppliers and the intended linear process becomes unreliable. Some supply chain risks in projects include lack of supplier commitment, poor order control, unexpected variations in lead time, critical material damaged in shipment and changes induced by suppliers and project members. These non-linear project risks have the potential to generate cumulative negative influences across the project.

In order to minimise such non-linear project risks related to the supply chain the basic concepts, skills and tools of supply chain management form essential support elements of project management. These basic concepts and tools are equally applicable to the success of operation management whether in manufacturing or services. There follow some examples of these concepts in supply chain management.

It is also evident that there is now increasing awareness among both practitioners (www.viasysweb.com) and academics (O'Brien, 2001) of applying appropriate supply chain principles in major projects. The most noticeable change in the last three decades is the introduction of information and communication technology with faster and more comprehensive systems to improve the efficiency of project supply chains from procurement to suppliers.

Case example: Airbus A380

The Airbus A380 was a double-deck, four-engine airliner manufactured by Airbus SAS. It first flew on 27 April 2005 from Toulouse in France. After well-publicised lengthy delays commercial flights did not seem likely before 2008.

Airbus spent two years grappling with the design of the A350 and A380 while archrival Boeing went ahead with producing its 787 Dreamliner, winning more than 400 orders for the plane, which was due to go into commercial service in 2008. Costly delays in the production of the A380 super jumbo and surging demand for Boeing's 787 rocked Airbus and its parent company, the European Aeronautic Defense and Space Company (EADS), which had three chief executives in the span of a single year. The 12 billion euro A380 super jumbo project was overbudget, as well as being over two years behind schedule. A decision by the US mail group FedEx to cancel its order for 10 Airbus 380s caused massive losses at EADS. A major partner in the project, BAE Systems, also sold its share in the project.

The problems facing EADS in the Airbus 380 project were many and complex. Analysts highlighted two problems at the forefront which were related to funding and supply chain management. For historical reasons manufacturing was a transnational process, structured around key manufacturing units in the UK (BAE Systems), Germany (Daimler-Chrysler Aerospace), France (Aerospace-Matra) and Spain (CASA). Each country was responsible for producing a complete section of the aircraft and then transporting it by a specially constructed roll-on/roll-off vessel (built by a shipyard in China) to the final assembly line in Toulouse. In addition the project had hundreds of suppliers, contractors and subcontractors (including Rolls-Royce, GE/Pratt & Whitney, Smiths Industries, Rockwell Collins and Northrop Grumman).

There may not have been simple solutions to the complex and serious problems of Airbus 380. However EADS recognised the link between project management and supply chain management and implemented project management methods and tools for suppliers. This allowed them to simultaneously manage resources, time, cost, and performance in order to ensure project success. In a structured course, chosen representatives for suppliers learnt and practised a straightforward and effective project management methodology that was adaptable to all types of projects.

Source: www.aerospace-technology.com/projects (2006)

WHAT ABOUT LOGISTICS MANAGEMENT?

Is there a difference between 'logistics' and 'supply chain' management? The Council of Logistics Management has recently changed its name to the Council of Supply Chain Management Professionals, which indicates that it sees logistics management as part of the supply chain process. When it was still the Council of Logistics Management, it defined logistics management as:

> *The process of planning, implementing and controlling the efficient, cost effective flow and storage of raw materials, in-process inventory, finished goods, and related information from point of origin to point of consumption for the purpose of conforming to customer requirements.*

Its new definition is:

> *Supply chain management encompasses the planning and management of all activities involved in sourcing and procurement, conversion, and all logistics management activities. Importantly, it also includes coordination and collaboration with channel partners, which can be suppliers, intermediaries, third party service providers, and customers. In essence, supply chain management integrates supply and demand management within and across companies.*
>
> > *(Council of Supply Chain Management Professionals, 2007;*
> > *http://cscmp.org)*

If we consider these definitions we see they are very similar to the earlier explanations we have provided (Swink et al. 2010 and Simchi-Levi et al. 2003) and can conclude that for our purposes, at least in a manufacturing and supply organisation, logistics and supply chain management are synonymous. If one is inclined to separate the physical movement of logistics in a service organisation, we can see that there is but a fine border between logistics and supply chain management in the service sector. Taylor (1997) goes on to divide supply chain management into:

1. Logistics and Supply Chain Strategy
2. Purchasing and Supplies Management
3. Manufacturing Logistics
4. Distribution Planning and Strategy
5. Warehouse Planning and Operations Management
6. Inventory Management
7. Transport Management
8. International Logistics and International Market Entry Strategies.

Taylor's definition infers that 'logistics' is a subset of 'SCM'. Each subtopic contributes to the performance of the overall supply chain process and, as a consequence, to improved stakeholder satisfaction.

WHAT ARE INBOUND AND OUTBOUND LOGISTICS?

The flow of information and physical goods from both customers and suppliers to the business or the conversion centre (e.g. a factory, a warehouse or an office) is termed 'inbound logistics'. Likewise the flow of information, goods or service from the conversion centre to the customer constitutes 'outbound logistics'. To put it more simply, inbound logistics relate to demand and procurement while outbound logistics concern supply and service. Figure 1.2 and Figure 1.3 show examples of inbound and outbound logistics in a foods factory.

Demand and supply planning capabilities enable companies to balance inbound and outbound logistics and thus to maximise return on assets and ensure a profitable match of supply and demand. Inbound and outbound logistics are also described as 'upstream' and 'downstream' processes. For example, Christopher (1992) defines supply chain management as the management of upstream and downstream relationships with suppliers and customers to deliver superior customer value at less cost to the supply chain as a whole.

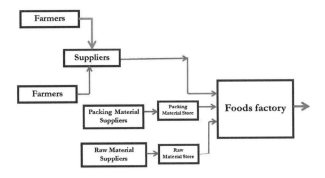

Figure 1.2   Inbound logistics

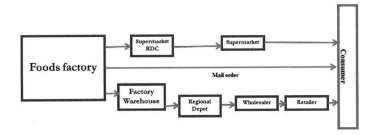

Figure 1.3   Outbound logistics

WHAT IS THE E-SUPPLY CHAIN?

As shown in Figure 1.1 the traditional supply chain was concerned with a linear flow of information and products or services from customers to suppliers through various stages of processes, while the information flow was the domain of the commercial division and the conversion process of materials flow was a manufacturing or technical division responsibility. During the 1990s the concept of Total Supply Chain Management shifted the responsibility for all elements of supply to operations management or supply chain management.

According to Basu (2002) the Internet-enabled integrated supply chain, or 'e-supply chain', has extended the linear flow of the supply chain to e-suppliers and systems or a supply web (see Figure 1.4). It now includes all customers, right down to the end user or consumer, suppliers' customers, customers' suppliers etc. The frontrunners of the new collaborative business model, such as Dell and Toyota, are sourcing materials and products in response to customer demand and minimising both inventory and dealers. The collaborative culture has enabled these companies to become adept at managing relationships between customers, suppliers and multidisciplinary company functions with a sharing of transparent information and knowledge exchange.

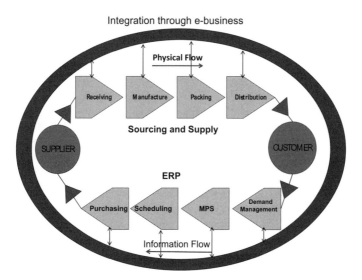

Figure 1.4   e-supply chain or e-web

HOW DO YOU BALANCE THE VOICE OF THE CUSTOMER (VOC) AND THE VOICE OF BUSINESS (VOB) IN SUPPLY CHAIN MANAGEMENT?

In any business or operation, a manager has to find a balance between the two conflicting objectives of demand from the customer and supply from operations. The voice of the customer (VOC) is articulated as customer service. Customer service is the primary objective of supply chain management. However, customer service has to be sustainable and balanced with the efficient use of resources. The secondary objective of supply chain management is to reduce costs and to make effective use of resources.

For simplicity, three key parameters of customer service are considered. These are Specification, Cost (or Price) and Timing. The customer expects the goods or service to be delivered according to acceptable standards, to be of an affordable price and to arrive on time. The relative importance of specification, cost and time could change depending on the market condition, competition and the desirability of demand. The second objective, to efficiently utilise resources to meet customer service requirements, is the voice of business (VOB). Given infinite resources, any system can provide adequate customer service, but many companies have gone out of business in spite of possessing satisfied customers (Wild, 2002). To provide a sustained and sustainable level of customer service efficiently the use of resources is essential. A starting point for balancing VOC and VOB is Resource Utilisation and Customer Service Analysis (RU/CS), which aims to determine the gaps between what is desired and what is actually feasible.

RU/CS analysis is a simple tool to establish the relative importance of the key parameters of both resource utilisation and customer service and to identify their conflicts. Wild (2002) suggests the starting point of the RU/CS analysis with the Operations Objectives Chart, as shown in Table 1.1. The relative importance of the key parameters for RU (i.e. machines, materials and labour) and CS (i.e. specification, cost and time) can be given a rating of 1, 2 or 3 (3 being the most important).

Table 1.1   Operations objectives chart

	Resource Utilisation			Customer Service		
	Machines	Materials	Labour	Specification	Cost	Time
Operation						

Consider a mail order company where customers are expecting good value for money and do not mind receiving goods from catalogues within a reasonable delivery time. The Operation Manager has focused on the utilisation of own resources to minimise operational costs. Figure 1.5 shows the ratings of objectives and actual performance, and highlights the misalignment. It is evident that further examination is required for timing and material.

As shown in Figure 1.6, there is a conflict between cost and materials and further attention or a change of policy is required to resolve this divergence.

When we study the apparently contradictory objectives of RU and CS we realise that they have one thing in common, that is cost and price. If we can reduce the cost of the production of goods or services by improved resource utilisation then we are in a better position to lessen the price to the customer.

RU/CS analysis does not provide solutions to the conflicts but identifies broad areas for attention. It is also important to note that the relative priorities of RU and CS can vary within the same business depending on the product and customer. To find solutions the supply chain manager will seek other tools, techniques and processes of supply chain management, which we shall explain in later chapters. One such process is Enterprise Resources Planning (ERP).

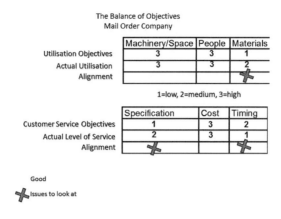

Figure 1.5   Balance of objectives

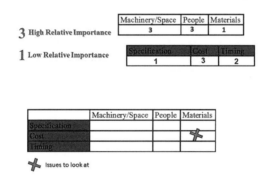

Figure 1.6   RU/CS analysis

WHAT IS ERP?

The business objective is to convert customer demand by optimising the utilisation of resources to deliver effective customer service. This applies to all organisations regardless of whether they are in the manufacturing or service sectors. Enterprise resources planning (ERP) systems provide a single up-to-date database incorporating manufacturing, finance and human resource applications extended to include the tracking of orders and inwards goods, work in progress and the delivery of finished goods. The system is accessible to all departments for the planning and execution of supply chain activities. Thus enterprise resources planning systems integrate (or attempt to integrate) all data and processes of an organisation into a single unified system in order to achieve integration.

The term ERP originally implied systems designed to plan the utilisation of enterprise-wide resources. Although the abbreviation ERP originated in the manufacturing environment as a successor to MRPII (Manufacturing Resources Planning), today's use of the term 'ERP systems' has much broader scope. ERP systems typically attempt to cover all basic functions of an organisation, regardless of that establishment's commerce or charter. Governments, businesses, not-for-profit organisations and other large entities all utilise ERP systems.

HOW DO YOU DELIVER VALUE IN SUPPLY CHAIN MANAGEMENT?

The delivery of goods and services of expected standards on time at the 'best in class' cost is creating value for money for customers and thus adding value to the business. An effective supply chain management team can deliver value by a Value Stream methodology or a total supply chain management approach.

The value stream system transcends the traditional manner of departmentalising stages of the business process. The value stream highlights the importance of the operations manager being involved in all aspects of the process – from supplier right through to the customer and, if possible, to the customer's customer. The 'old' method was that one department or function would be responsible for purchasing goods and services, another for planning. The scheduling of activities was often a separate task, as was warehousing and distribution, and operations were just one step in the whole process of providing services. With the value stream approach, functional boundaries are ignored and in many organisations it is now accepted that the operations manager has to control the total process, from purchasing input goods and services to the final stage of satisfying the customer. Marketing, accounting, human resources and other support functions do not show up on the value stream as such, but operations managers must be vitally interested and involved in these internal operations of the organisation.

The value stream approach in supply chain aligns well with Porter's (1985) value chain as shown in Figure 1.7. The idea of the value chain is based on the process view of organisations: the concept of seeing a manufacturing (or service) organisation as a system made up of subsystems, each with inputs, transformation processes and outputs. How value chain activities are carried out determines costs and affects profits.

Figure 1.7   Porter's value chain (reproduced from page 275, *Total Operations Solutions*, R. Basu and J.N. Wright, 2005)

Most organisations engage in hundreds, even thousands, of activities in the process of converting inputs to outputs. These actions can be classified generally as either primary or support activities that all businesses must undertake in some form. According to Porter (1985), the primary activities are:

1. **Inbound logistics** – involve relationships with suppliers and include all the activities required to receive, store, and disseminate inputs.
2. **Operations** – are all the activities required to transform inputs into outputs (products and services).
3. **Outbound logistics** – include all the activities required to collect, store, and distribute the output.
4. **Marketing and sales** – activities inform buyers about products and services, induce buyers to purchase them and facilitate their purchase.
5. **Service** – includes all the activities required to keep the product or service working effectively for the buyer after it is sold and delivered.

Secondary activities are:

1. **Infrastructure** – serves the company's needs and ties its various parts together. It consists of functions or departments such as accounting, legal, finance, planning, public affairs, government relations, quality assurance and general management.
2. **Procurement** – is the acquisition of inputs, or resources, for the firm.
3. **Human Resources Management** – consists of all activities involved in recruiting, hiring, training, developing, compensating and (if necessary) dismissing or laying off personnel.
4. **Technological development** – pertains to the equipment, hardware, software, procedures and technical knowledge brought to bear in a firm's transformation of inputs into outputs.

The success of a supply chain could be synonymous with the success of the value stream approach or the total supply chain method underpinned by the interaction between three key groups of players. These are the customers, external suppliers and the departments involved with the primary and secondary activities of the organisation.

The customer is the focus of any organisation. Churchill once said that war is too important to be left to the generals, and the same can be said of marketing. Marketing is too important to be left to the marketing department. Everyone in an organisation should be vitally interested in marketing that organisation. Nonetheless, it is the function of the marketing department to *know* what the customer wants and what the competition is doing or is likely to do. Marketing specifies the product and its attributes. These qualities may range from the essential down to the desirable, and perhaps include extras that the customer does not even want. As well as defining the product or service to be offered, marketing has to establish the price, forecast demand and have a say in how the product or service will be distributed or delivered. Finally they are responsible for promotion with the aim of stimulating demand. Marketing also has to sell the product/service internally within the firm to the operations and other functions of the organisation. In fact, it can be said that marketing is the link between the market and customers and operations.

In some organisations suppliers are treated with distrust, and the business strategy adopted is to shop around and to get the best deal on each occasion. In these types of establishments information is not shared with suppliers. When orders are placed the supplier is not told what the purpose of that order is, and thus is not in a position to advise, even if they were so inclined, of any alternative products or new technology. With this approach little loyalty is shown to any supplier – indeed, the supplier is almost treated as an adversary.

The value stream approach is to view key suppliers of goods and services as part of the team, to share information and to seek advice. Key suppliers are those that are important to the smooth operation of the system. In some cases the supplier can become involved in the day-to-day operations of the organisation, and might also be expected to advise and to assist in product development. Cost no longer becomes the key issue. Instead of price alone, suppliers will be judged on their loyalty and ability to deliver goods and services to the required standard and on time. Suppliers can also become part of the information-gathering arm of the organisation; often they have a different perspective as to what the competition are up to (changes in buying patterns, timetables, new packaging, use of new materials etc.). Suppliers are also in a good position to offer technical advice regarding new technology and alternative materials.

Communication between departments (especially marketing, operations and logistics) within an organisation has to be two-way and must be aimed at helping rather than as a means of apportioning blame or criticising. With traditional hierarchical organisations a 'bunker' mentality can develop whereby each function is walled off from the other, and any suggestion, no matter how helpful, is taken as a threat or a challenge. World-class organisations are noted by the manner in which the figurative brick walls that separate functions have been broken down, and by the teamwork that exists between all roles to achieve the common aspiration. This requires that everyone in the organisation knows what the goals and objectives are and that the culture is conducive to the enthusiastic pursuit of the targets for the common good of the whole, rather than for the specific interests of one department. Information is open to all, and there are no secrets.

SUPPLIER PARTNERSHIP

Reviewing the impact of new technologies on supply chain provides an interesting development of partnering with suppliers. As indicated earlier, in the past many manufacturers regarded their suppliers with some suspicion, almost as opponents. Little loyalty was shown to the suppliers and consequently the supplier was never certain as to their future relationship with an organisation. Often the purchasing or procurement department would see their role as screwing the best deal possible from a supplier.

The huge growth in outsourcing and, more importantly, online access to information via the Internet have changed that. Companies have realised that achieving world-class excellence in their own sites is not enough. It is important to raise the standards of suppliers as well as learn from them by working in partnership with them. The tightly controlled service level agreements are being replaced by joint service agreements with the free exchange of data and knowledge. The approach is changed from coordination to cooperation However, the success of any benefits will depend on mutual trust, a highly developed commercial relationship and an efficient system of data exchange.

In order to improve the effectiveness of data exchange, companies are sharing with their suppliers (and customers) common systems such as European Article Numbering (EAN) standards, Electronic Data Interchange (EDI) and web-based Extranets. For example EDI enables companies to communicate with each other. Purchase orders to suppliers can be eliminated by using customers' order schedules. Moreover by EDI and Extranets the supplier could be authorised to link directly into the manufacturer's MRPII or ERP system. The emergence of Internet protocol has helped the interaction between powerful supply chain systems such as i2, Manugistics, Ariba, Oracle and SAP/R3.

TOTAL SUPPLY CHAIN MANAGEMENT WITHIN PROJECTS

Our analysis of the key factors and new developments in supply chain management clearly indicates one thing. Focusing on the conventional practices of supply chain management within the organisation (such as forecasting, capacity planning, inventory management, scheduling and distribution management) may achieve operational excellence within the confines of an individual business organisation. However it will offer only a partial solution to optimising customer service. It can be compared with sitting in a high-performance motor car in a traffic jam – the sound system and air conditioning might be state of the art but the overall travel experience is not great. Likewise, what is the point of having a perfect stainless steel link within a rusty chain? Unless the whole process is efficient the individual unit cannot achieve its potential.

It is therefore vital for any organisation or a major project, being more and more dependent on both local and global outside resources and information, to work in harmony with all stakeholders of the supply chain – including customers and suppliers. We need a holistic value stream approach to supply chain or a total supply chain management approach in supervising a major project.

Building on the experience of the holistic model for total supply chain management (Basu and Wright, 2008) a model for project supply chain management has been developed comprising six building blocks, as follows:

- Customer focus and stakeholders
- Resources and time management
- Procurement and supplier focus
- Supply management
- Building and installation
- Handover and closure.

These building blocks are integrated by three cross-functional processes as follows:

- Systems and procedures
- Regular reviews
- Quality and performance management.

The building blocks of project supply are further explained in Chapter 2. The importance of the total supply chain approach in a major project can also be evaluated by Value Stream Mapping (Basu, 2009, p. 122). Value stream mapping (VSM) is a visual illustration of all the activities required to bring a product through the main flow, from raw material to the stage of reaching the customer. According to Womack and Jones (1998), the initial objective of creating a value stream map is to identify every action required to make a specific product.

SUMMARY

The primary purpose of this introductory chapter was to provide an overview of supply chain management principles. It aimed to indicate how an effective supply chain management process adds value to all types of businesses, whether in the manufacturing or service sectors, public or not-for-profit organisations and also to projects. It also seeks to initiate the understanding of some core concepts of the book, including the tenet that it is people, not processes or technology that make things happen. It is critical to have data sharing and interaction between all stakeholders in the total supply chain using a value stream 'total supply chain' approach.

Supply chain management constitutes a critical knowledge and tool set for any project management team. The adequate application of the knowledge base, tools and skill sets can assist the project team's delivery of the product or service on time, on budget and at an acceptable level of quality. However, it should be emphasised that project supply chain is not just the procurement of goods and services. The following chapters will illustrate just how to 'make it happen'.

CHAPTER 2

THE BUILDING BLOCKS OF A PROJECT SUPPLY CHAIN

INTRODUCTION

In Chapter 1 we discussed the need for a Total Supply Chain Management approach and introduced the concepts of building blocks. The importance of each building block is explained in this chapter. No block stands alone but, rather, each is a component of the whole. In combination these bricks show the activities, stages and processes of the extended supply chain. The sequence of practices creates a flow between different stages to fulfil a customer's need for a product or service. Therefore we aim to explain in this chapter:

1. What are the building blocks of a Project Supply Chain?
2. Are all the building blocks suited to every project?

WHAT ARE THE BUILDING BLOCKS OF A PROJECT SUPPLY CHAIN?

It is important that a 'total supply chain management approach' is applied and all the building blocks of the supply chain are examined. The synergy that results from the benefits contributed by all elements as a whole far exceeds the aggregate of gains achieved for an individual element. The integrated approach is truly more than the sum of its parts. If one concentrates exclusively on isolated areas, a false impression may be inevitable and inappropriate action taken.

This maxim can be illustrated by the Indian folk tale of four blind men who were confronted with a new phenomenon – an elephant! As none of the men could see what was in front of them, each tried to ascertain the situation in their own way. The first man, by touching its ear, assumed that the elephant was a fan. A second was hit by the elephant's tail and concluded that it was a whip. The third man bumped into a leg and thought it was a column, while the fourth, on holding the trunk, decided that it was an over-sized hose. Each man, on the evidence he had, came to a logical conclusion. However their deductions were the result of looking at only partial data and in fact all had made an erroneous judgement by failing to construe that the total object was an elephant. As with all feedback devices where a basic message is given, inferences and decisions may be drawn from isolated data which will be false and misleading.

A story in a business context will further underline the limitation of tackling only one part of the whole problem. Following attending a conference, the project director of a multinational company, decided that Earned Value Management (EVM) must be the best way forward in a major project. So he organised his project team, called in experts from a big consulting firm and set up an earned value management training programme. The team did an excellent job on two labour-intensive work packages by systematically reviewing Earned Values, Planned Values and Actual Spends at the critical stages of those work packages. As a result the two enterprises were progressing well and fortunately both were on time and in budget. However, it soon transpired that it was very difficult to estimate the planned values and actual spends of many critical work packages governed by procurement schedules. Furthermore, EVM failed to take into account the impact of risks and issues related to quality and safety. Therefore, in isolation the EVM programmes did not improve the overall performance of Project Management.

As we mentioned in Chapter 1, our model for total supply chain management comprises six building block configurations, viz:

- Customer focus and stakeholders
- Resources and time management
- Procurement and supplier focus
- Supply and stock management
- Building and installation
- Handover and closure.

In addition there are three cross-functional integrating processes:

- Systems and procedures
- Regular reviews
- Quality and performance management.

This model is illustrated in Figure 2.1. Each of the building blocks is briefly described below.

It is also important to point out that there are three streams or categories in Figure 2.1, depending on the affinity of the building blocks. These are:

a) Project Planning Chain: in this stream the building blocks are dealing with project planning activities and information flow. The building blocks in this stream are:

- Customer focus and stakeholders
- Resources and time management
- Procurement and supplier focus.

b) Project Delivery Chain: here, the building blocks relate to the project implementation and closure activities and physical flow of materials on site. The building blocks in this stream are:

- Supply management
- Building and installation
- Handover and closure.

c) Project Integration: at this stage the building components of project supply chain are acting as the integrators of other building blocks at various stages of the project life cycle. The building components in this stream are:

- Systems and procedures
- Regular reviews
- Quality and performance management.

Each of the project supply chain building blocks, described briefly below, will be covered in more detail in Chapters 3, 4, 5, 6 and 7 as part of the above three streams.

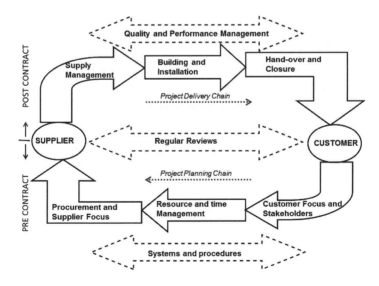

Figure 2.1   Project supply chain building blocks

Customer Focus and Stakeholders

Customers exist both at the start and end of the supply chain. A customer is the person who is paying for the goods or services or is most affected by the outcome of the process. In a project supply chain a customer could be a sponsor, an investor or an end user. Let us not forget that the demand for a product or service is created by customers.

The basis of all supply chain planning and decisions is underpinned by the forecast of future demand. A supply chain process cannot exist without knowledge and planning for the future. All 'push' processes are executed in anticipation of customer demand and all 'pull' processes are carried out in response to customer demand. It is a misconception that demand forecast is not required in a pull or just-in-time procedure. Without a forecast of future demand in a pull system, a manager cannot plan the capacity and have the resources required to respond to a customer order. For a traditional push process a manager arranges the level of production and capacity based on the forecast of future demand. Even in a service industry, where the demand is not discrete, business planning will be unsatisfactory without an estimate of future requirement. In a not-for-profit organisation, demand is unpredictable but it does have customers and it has a core budget based on demand forecast.

In all instances of a supply chain the first step is to forecast what the customer exigency will be in the future. It is important to note that is not possible to produce a perfect forecast as there are so many variables affecting a future demand – such as past need, promotion and advertising of the product, market share, state of the economy, price discounts, competition and the introduction of new products. Peter Drucker once said, 'The best way to predict the future is to create it.' There are also some recognised characteristics of forecasts: e.g. there will always be a forecast error, longer-term predictions are less accurate than short-term estimates and aggregate projections are usually more accurate than individual calculations. In a project supply chain also the importance of demand forecasts cannot be underrated. Without a good forecast or materials, resources and third party services the forward planning of resources and procurement schedules would be inadequate and expensive.

It is recognised that a critical determinant of project success is agreeing the success criteria with key stakeholders before any design or planning activity. Stakeholders comprise many people, in addition to customers, whose lives are affected by the outcomes of the project. The demand forecast actually depends on project deliverables. This is due to the fact that the outcomes are project deliverables and they determine the success criteria. Therefore the demand forecast is also dependent on the agreement with key stakeholders.

Resources and Time Management

A primary objective of supply chain management is to optimise supply capacity to fulfil demand in time. In the real world, resources are not infinite. Satisfying customers on time can be crucial. However an increase in capacity is expensive, be it machines and equipment, warehouse space, transport, stocks of input materials and finished product, or, of course, people. Therefore a supply chain manager must make decisions regarding capacity levels and buffer them to meet the variation in demand. This can be achieved either by adjusting capacity or production in order to hold output stocks of goods. An organisation may provide excess capacity to satisfy demands for peak periods or set an upper limit of the capacity based on the average demand. This allows them to balance the cost of holding excess inventory on one hand or losing sales on the other.

There are a few options for capacity optimisation open to a manager and there are proven processes to assist him or her. One such process is aggregate planning, where an organisation determines levels of capacity, production and inventory over a planning horizon to maximise the profit. Another established process in operations management is Enterprise Resource Planning (ERP), which has evolved from Materials Requirement Planning (MRP) and Manufacturing Resource Planning (MRPII). ERP is closely linked with Sales and Operations Planning (S&OP) and comprises a series of sequential processes by using a single set of databases – viz. demand planning, rough cut capacity planning, master operations scheduling, materials requirement preparation, detailed capacity planning, purchase scheduling and production scheduling. Number crunching is done using a computer system such as SAP R/3. The success of ERP depends on the structured review process by planners, managers and users.

In project management, Critical Path Scheduling and Earned Value Management are popular tools for assigning resources and time. The planning processes are supported by software such as Microsoft® Project and Oracle® Primavera. However the application of ERP in major projects is now assisting resources planning and procurement schedules and is interfaced with Enterprise Project Management (EPM) systems.

Procurement and Supplier Focus

Project procurement is often considered the focal point of project supply chain and the supply chain manager is usually selected from a procurement background. The procurement activities in projects have two main subdivisions: the buying of materials and placing contracts with suppliers and contractors. Hence procurement and supplier focus are interconnected. The optimisation of internal capacity can be supplemented by buying in external capacity and resources. As Reid and Sanders (2002) say: 'Make or buy is a type of backward integration decision, where the company decides whether to purchase certain materials or tasks or perform the operation itself. Often this is called outsourcing. Many companies routinely out-source certain services, such as janitorial services, repair, security, payroll, or records management' (p. 56). For the supply chain, the procurement of external capacity and resource could include packaging materials, part built-up assemblies, contracting out utilities and maintenance, hiring contract or casual labour, selecting approved suppliers and outsourcing. An example of part built-up assemblies is where an American car typically consists of 25,000 components to be constructed on the manufacturing line, while a Japanese car of a similar class might only consist of 12,000.

In a typical manufacturing organisation the cost of bought-in resources accounts for 60 to 90 per cent of the cost of goods sold (COGS). Thus a powerful way to improve shareholder returns is to address the reduction of purchasing costs. A proper purchasing and supply management also in a project can give a network of suppliers capable of delivering service quality. At the same time, this will allow them to beat competitors, in addition to securing cost reduction over a period. In a market-driven competitive world, businesses are continuously seeking new suppliers and partners, including outsourcing.

The Internet has provided new challenges and potential solutions and has enabled extensive connectivity. These new capabilities of e-commerce offer the facility for supply chain partners to share information in real time. Companies have now recognised that great improvements in value can be attained by coordinating and cooperating the efforts along the supply chain. These real-time advantages of the Internet are now being achieved in major projects. In short, projects that collaborate, sharing plans and information, are able to improve the overall supply chain performance to their mutual benefit.

The development of a professional service industry has also in recent years increased considerably; however, as observed by Mitchell (1998), purchasing teams appear to have made less effort to reduce costs by outsourcing services. Nonetheless the importance of service level agreements and supplier partnerships is growing in the global supply chain. A survey by Wade (2003) showed that 31 per cent of the total procurement cost is for bought-in services.

The selection of appropriate or preferred suppliers should involve alternative and complementary attributes between those suppliers and the receiving organisation. Slack et al. (2006) suggest four basic capabilities to make sensible trade-offs:

- Technical capability – the product or service knowledge to deliver sustainable quality
- Operations capability – the process knowledge to ensure effective supply

- Financial capability – the financial strength to fund the business
- Managerial capability – the management talent to develop future business.

It is important to raise the standards of suppliers as well as to learn from them by working in partnership with them. Tightly controlled service level contracts are being replaced by joint service agreements with the free exchange of data and knowledge. Success will depend on mutual trust, a highly developed commercial relationship and an efficient system of data exchange.

Supply Management

Physical inventory – whether equipment or material – must be controlled in projects. Although this is an area of neglect in many undertakings, the good practice of operations in assets and stock management should be applied to projects. The purpose of inventories or stocks in operations is to buffer against variations in demand and supply. Inventories usually reside in three stages of a manufacturing process: input stocks (e.g. raw and packaging materials); process stocks (e.g. semi-finished products); and output stocks (e.g. finished products). Wild (2002) introduced the concept of consumed and non-consumed stocks. Consumed articles (such as materials or products) are used by the process or customers and must be replenished in shorter cycles. Non-consumed items (for instance capital equipment and labour) are repeatedly used by the process, needing repair and maintenance, and are replaced at longer intervals.

Inventories could be allocated either by design or can accumulate as a result of poor planning and scheduling. Generally inventory is viewed as a negative impact on business, incurring the costs of capital (interest paid or interest foregone), storage space, handling, insurance, increased risk of damage and theft, and obsolescence. On the other hand, lack of inventory leads to lost production in the factory and unrealised sales at the end of the supply chain. Holding an inventory of materials and finished products can be seen as an insurance against the uncertainty of supply and a means to overcome unforeseen variations in demand.

Inventory management is a good indicator of the effectiveness of supply chain management. It is relatively easy to achieve higher levels of customer service by accumulating excessive stocks. It will also obscure short-term operational problems. But this is a costly and risky option in terms of cash flow. Obsolete inventory – be it caused by changes in technology, fashion or due to foodstuffs past their use-by date – clearly has little salvage value. Therefore it is vital to optimise the inventory level.

In thus optimising inventory levels, two types of stocks are considered: cycle stock and safety stock. Firstly, cycle stock depends on costs associated with ordering, transportation, quantity discount, lead times from suppliers and customer demand.

On the other hand, safety stock is the buffer against the variation of demand during the lead time and depends on forecast accuracy, the reliability of suppliers and customer service level.

Project Managers might have a nonchalant attitude towards inventories, but not so for Accountants. The deliveries from suppliers, whether material or equipment, must be received, inspected and possibly stored before use. The same attention to records and the control of goods from external suppliers should also be applied to internal suppliers.

Building and Installation Management

In a project supply chain, 'building and installation' is the building block that makes things happen. It is where plans are executed in sites and facilities to produce goods or services for customers. This stage is comparable to operations management in manufacturing industries. Operations Management is the activity of managing resources and processes that produce goods and services. Input resources (viz. information, materials and utilities) are transformed by three converting components (people, process and technology) into the desired outputs. Along with distribution management, operations management accounts for the physical flow of the supply chain; however most texts on operations management give only scant coverage to the topic of supply chain management.

Operations exist in all types of supply chain, whether it is for delivering a product or a service: a popular perception of an operation is that it is where physical activities or transformations are involved, e.g. manufacturing. If you think that you do not have an operation if you are involved, e.g. in the field of sales and marketing, banking or insurance, or the health service or charity organisations, then you are incorrect. In actual fact you will always have an operation as long as you use resources to produce products, services or a mixture of both. In other words, if you have input, process and output – you have an operation.

During the 1960s and earlier, operations management was exclusively the domain of the manufacturing industries. Since the 1970s it has been used in both the manufacturing and service sectors, and it also implies that a service operation can be decoupled as repetitive and non-repetitive operations and that manufacturing principles and techniques can be applied to repetitive service operations. More recently the term 'operations and process management' has been used to cover all parts of the organisation. For clarity, in the context of this book operations management will include all types or parts of organisations.

Handover and Closure

There is no doubt that supply chain order fulfilment is the Achilles heel of the e-business economy. At the end of every e-commerce, online trading and virtual supply chain there is a factory, a warehouse and a transport. The Internet has elevated the performance of information accessibility, currency transactions and data accuracy; but the real effectiveness of supply chain from the source to customer cannot be achieved without the physical efficiency of the supply chain.

In the context of project management, the final handover and closure process determines the success and sustainability of project outcomes. The skill with which the closure is managed has a great deal to do with the quality of life after the project. A successful closure is the destination of the project supply chain. The closure stage of the project may have less impact on technical success or failure, but it has huge influence on the residual attitudes of the client and end users toward the project.

Systems and Procedures

Systems and procedures are essential components to integrate the building block configurations of the total supply chain. There are three major categories of systems and procedures:

- External regulatory and internal quality standards
- Financial and accounting procedures
- Information and communication technology.

The activities of a supply chain are affected by both national and international regulatory requirements on packaging, storage, pallets, vehicles, working hours, tariffs and many other issues. In addition an organisation maintains its own quality standards and service level agreements with its suppliers and partners. The bodies of knowledge and project methodologies such as PMBOK (2008) and PRINCE2 (2009) are powerful guidelines to integrating the building blocks of project supply chain in order to successfully deliver a project.

Another important issue is improving the financial performance of the company. Under pressure to participate in fashionable improvement activities, or to become involved in the newest business wisdom, management may lose sight of the real issue – improving profitability. In response to pressures from stakeholders there is a risk of overemphasis on short-term financial performance. Consequently this myopic approach results in overinvestment in short-term fixers and underinvestment in longer-term development plans. There is a need for a balanced approach.

The Internet, now taken for granted, has seen the use of technologies to create electronic communication networks within and between organisations and individuals. The implementation of Enterprise Resource Planning (ERP), websites, e-commerce, electronic data interchange and email systems has transformed the process of the exchange of ideas. It has allowed individuals within organisations, and both business-to-business as well as business-to-customer, to communicate freely together and to share data in 'real time'. Information Technology (IT) has now grown into Information and Communication Technology (ICT). In this ICT domain we consider two broad areas:

- Information technology and systems
- E-business.

There is a visible absence of a dedicated chapter on systems and procedures in the published books on supply chain management, which this volume aims to rectify.

Regular Reviews

Regular reviews of project supply chain are comparable to sales and operations planning (S&OP) in operations management. Sales and operations planning is a cross-functional management review process to integrate the activities of the total supply chain. The classical concept of sales and operations planning is rooted to the Manufacturing Resource Planning (MRPII) process. In basic S&OP, the company operating plan (comprising sales forecast, production plan, inventory plan and shipments) is updated on a regular monthly basis by the senior management of a manufacturing organisation. The virtues, application and training of S&OP have been promoted by Oliver Wight Associates (see Ling and Goddard, 1988) since the early 1970s.

Project review gatherings are held regularly, and their frequency and participation depend on the type of meeting. Project team meetings by work packages or task groups are generally held every week and led by the Team Manager. Project progress groups (also known as 'gateway' review meetings) usually take place every month and are led by the project manager. Milestone review meetings are convened at predetermined dates and participated by the Project Board and project manager. In addition ad hoc review groups (e.g. pre-audit, health safety and environment etc.) are also scheduled with specific agenda.

Quality and Performance Management

Quality and performance management acts both as a driving force of improvement and a fact-based integrating agent to support the planning, operations and review processes. The foundation of performance management is rooted in quality management principles supported by key performance indicators.

There are many different definitions and dimensions of quality to be found in books and academic literature. Basu (2004) defines quality with three dimensions, such as design quality (specification), process quality (conformance) and organisation quality (sustainability). When an organisation develops and defines its quality strategy, it is important to share a common definition of quality, and each department within a company can work towards a common objective. The product quality should contain defined attributes of both numeric specifications and perceived dimensions. The process quality, whether it relates to manufacturing or service operations, should also comprise some defined criteria of acceptable service levels so that the conformity of the output can be validated against these criteria. Perhaps the most important determinant of how we perceive sustainable quality is the functional and holistic role we fulfil within the establishment. It is only when an organisation begins to change its approach to a holistic culture, emphasising a single set of numbers based on transparent measurement with senior management commitment, that the 'organisation quality' germinates.

A good reference line of key performance indicators of a supply chain is the 'Balanced Scorecard' by Kaplan and Norton (2004). Kaplan and Norton argue that 'a valuation of intangible assets and company capabilities would be especially helpful since, for information age companies, these assets are more critical to success than tradition al physical and tangible assets' (p. 52). The Balanced Scorecard retains traditional financial measures, customer services and resource utilisation (Internal Business Process) and includes additional measures for learning (people) and growth (innovation). This approach complements measures of past performance with drivers for future development.

ARE ALL THE BUILDING BLOCKS SUITED TO ALL PROJECTS?

The objectives of supply chain management – to balance the demand and supply for the right product or service on time and at an affordable price – remain the same for all businesses. However it is also true that supply chains serving different markets should be managed in different ways. Both Fisher (1997) and Christopher (2000) have drawn the distinction between 'lean supply chain' and 'agile supply chain'. Agility should not be confused with lean or leanness. 'Lean' is about doing more with less, often with minimum inventory and by placing the emphasis on efficiency. On the other hand, the key characteristics of an 'agile' supply chain include responsiveness and flexibility.

As shown in Figure 2.2 the approaches for an agile or lean supply chain are determined by the volume and variety/variability. An agile supply chain responds quickly to changes in demand – whether this is caused by a low volume for high variety products or the unpredictability of demand. By contrast a lean supply chain works very efficiently when the volume is high and variability is

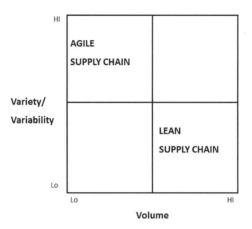

Figure 2.2   Lean and agile supply chain (reproduced from page 228, *Total Supply Chain Management*, R. Basu and J.N. Wright, 2008)

low. The occasions for a purely agile or purely lean supply chain are likely to be infrequent. It is a popular perception, though not always validated, that functional or commodity products need a lean supply chain and innovative and new products require agile supply chain management. As Christopher (2000) points out, there will often be situations for a 'hybrid strategy' where a combination of the two may be appropriate.

Our building blocks of the total supply chain will apply to both lean and agile supply chains, but their end objectives require different ways of using these building blocks. In a lean supply chain, emphasis will be on accurate demand and capacity planning, keeping the inventory low and running the plant efficiently. However in an agile supply chain the weight will be given to high service levels by responding rapidly to the end customers. This will require flexibility in process and plant capacity and a higher inventory, usually of semi-finished products, nearer the demand point.

The supply chain in the service sector will also need all the building blocks of the total supply chain, although they should be used and managed differently depending on services. For example in an insurance service industry the approach to inventory management would be different from that adopted in an automobile manufacturing business. In the service sector the variation in demand is buffered by managing 'non-consumed' stock (such as people and databases), while in the manufacturing sector the emphasis is on consumed stock (e.g. materials).

PROJECT SUPPLY CHAIN BUILDING BLOCKS AND PROJECT LIFE CYCLE

The life cycle of a project (Figure 2.3) typically goes through four stages, viz. initiation, design, execution and closure (Turner, 1999). It is important to note, as shown in Figure 2.4, that these four aspects of project life cycle are also in congruence with the eight processes of PRINCE2 (2009). The nomenclature of each phase of the project life cycle often varies from Turner's given names in many project applications (e.g. definition, design, implementation and handover) or it may have more stages (e.g. concept, feasibility, implementation, operation and termination in BS 6079). However alternative periods of project life cycle can be easily aligned to Turner's given names. Hence the 'building blocks' of the project supply chain is aligned to Turner's project life cycle as shown in Figure 2.5.

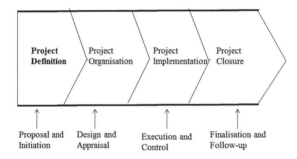

Figure 2.3   Project life cycle (with kind permission of Rodney Turner)

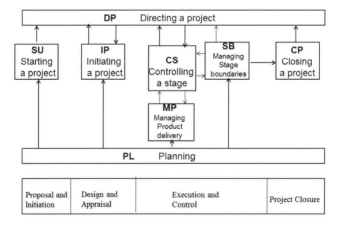

Figure 2.4   PRINCE2 and project life cycle

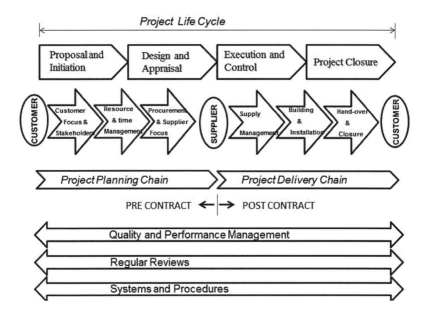

Figure 2.5   Project supply chain building blocks and project life cycle

In Figure 2.5 project supply chain building blocks have been presented as an 'open bracelet' against the four stages of the project life cycle. The building blocks of the project planning chain (viz. customer focus and stakeholders, resources and time management and procurement and supplier focus) align with the first two stages of project life cycle (proposal and initiation, design and appraisal). The project planning chain constitutes 'pre-contract' planning activities managed by the customer of the project, often referred to as the 'Intelligent Client' (APM, 2006). The project delivery chain encompasses 'post-contract' delivery activities managed by a consortium of main suppliers and contractors in collaboration with the customer or client. The integrating functions (systems and procedures, quality and performance management and regular reviews) span all building blocks of the project supply chain and the four stages of the project life cycle.

SUMMARY

In this chapter we have explained the characteristics and roles of supply chain building blocks in total supply chain management. The building blocks consist of nine components, out of which six are for supply chain configuration (customer focus and stakeholders, resources and time management, procurement and supplier focus, supply management, building and installation and handover and closure). Three components are for supply chain integration (systems and procedures, quality management and regular reviews). These building blocks will be applicable, to a varying degree, to all types and strategies of supply chains regardless of whether they are primarily pull or push processes, agile or lean supply chains or if in they are within the construction, manufacturing, technology or service sector of projects.

CHAPTER 3

PROJECT PLANNING CHAIN

INTRODUCTION

Supply Chain Management planning, methodologies and methods are key to ensuring that project resources arrive as required. The three building blocks of the Project Planning Chain provide a perspective to help make this happen (see Figure 2.1), viz:

1. Customer focus and stakeholders
2. Resources and time management
3. Procurement and supplier focus.

Projects are novel endeavours as they are undertaken to build up and deliver new development objectives. These may relate to infrastructure, products or systems. The process of development comes before delivery and it is undertaken by the product planning chain. This establishment is set up during the Initiation and Design stages of the project life cycle by the Sponsor or the Customer of the project. It is the sponsor or customer who seeks the assistance of Consultants at the project planning chain (during the initiation and design phases) and who depends mostly on Major Suppliers and Contractors at the Project Delivery Chain (during the Implementation and Closure phases). The sponsors or customers who collaborate well with their partners are known as 'Intelligent Clients'. The behaviour that characterises an intelligent client reflects the true nature of the relationship between partners in delivery, how the supply chain is managed, the role of contracts and who owns risk, uncertainty and opportunities (www.som.cranfield.ac.uk). This chapter describes the key activities and processes under the three building blocks of the project planning chain.

CUSTOMER FOCUS AND STAKEHOLDERS

Customer focus and stakeholders is the first of our six building blocks for project supply chain management. A customer could be a consumer (end user) or a sponsor, but ultimately the ownership of the project is determined by the organisation that provides the funding of the project.

The stakeholder is defined as person, group or organisation that has a direct or indirect stake in a project because it can affect or be affected by the outcome of that project. Key stakeholders at the initial stage of a task include creditors, sponsors, customers, directors, employees, the government (and its agencies), owners (shareholders) and investors from which the project draws its resources.

This building block ties in closely with the project definition and initiation. It goes without saying that the success of a project is critically dependent on more attention being paid to planning at its early stages. From the standpoint of supply chain management it is good practice to focus especially on three aspects: ·

1. Scope management
2. Stakeholder management
3. Supply chain management awareness.

Scope Management

Common problems in the administration of projects are the overrun in time and budget and the failure to realise and fully achieve the original scope of the project. In general, all ventures encompass four basic elements: scope, time, budget and quality. The traditional 'iron triangle' of project management comprises time, cost (budget) and quality. Subsidiary to these and cutting across all four are several areas as identified by Turner (1999). These consist of:

*   Work breakdown (activities)
*   Milestones
*   Responsibilities
*   Cost estimation
*   The control of costs
*   Estimation of time
*   Scheduling time and resource
*   Controlling time
*   Risk identification and management
*   Controlling risk
*   Balancing objectives, execution and control
*   Finalisation and close out
*   Follow-up after handover
*   Team leadership and administration
*   The choice of information system.

It is therefore vital that the Terms of Reference establish the overall scope, budget and time frame, i.e. the three key elements of the project. The Brief or the Project Initiation Document (PRINCE2, 2009) follows the terms of reference and gives them depth. The suggested contents of a Project Initiation Document (PID) include:

- Project scope
- Business case
- Team structure
- Project approach
- Project quality
- Risk log
- Project control
- Communication plan
- Time plan
- Next stage plan.

The terms of reference provide what is required, while the brief identifies what has to be done to make the project happen (Turner, 1999). The requirements of the brief are reasonably accurate estimates of resources and key steps or tasks as well as the skills required for each phase. The brief will also endeavour to establish cost, time and precedence for each stage. It is likely that it will also consider responsibilities and authority for the supply of resources. The Brief should not be limited to the above but must include any issue that will affect the successful outcome of the project, such as establishing stakeholders. Once stakeholders are identified, especially those who are not enthusiastic about the outcome, the seasoned Project Manager will seek to establish what the concerns are and if possible to reassure them or to find ways around their apprehensions (Turner, 1999).

All of the above, especially the brief, are based on estimates. By definition each project is unique, and seldom can any planned activity be taken as a certainty. It is a recognised fact that many Information Technology type projects are not completed as per the original terms of reference – indeed many are never completed at all. A well-published example is the UK government's undertaking to introduce smart cards for social welfare beneficiaries. This project ran for several years and was finally abandoned in 2000 at a cost, according to the National Audit Office, of £1 billion to the British taxpayers. At the time the scheme was cancelled it was said that even the first three months' target had not been achieved. The very valid reasons given by project managers for these types of failure are often:

- The client didn't know what they really wanted.
- The client kept on changing their mind and adding extra features.

In reply the customer could well say that the project manager did not listen and/ or understand the customer's needs. The truth will be somewhat greyer: there will be imperfections on both sides due to imperfect communication. Irrespective of who is at fault when things go wrong, ultimately it is the reputation of the project manager that will be at stake.

For a short-term project such as building a house, no matter how carefully the plans have been drawn up to meet the client's wishes, once construction begins the client will see that an additional window would make sense, or that a door has to be moved etc. After all, a plan is one-dimensional, and reality takes on a different perspective once that paper plan begins to transform into a three-dimensional product. Such changes, if agreed on early enough, will not cause problems for the builder and should not add appreciably to the cost. For longer-term schemes such as the British government's beneficiary payment proposal or the Crossrail Project, over time the sponsor will not only change their requirements, but the client representatives that the project manager has been dealing with will move on to be replaced by a new group.

Firstly, it is assumed that the project has been properly constituted with the appropriate signed-off terms of reference supported by a PID, where the scope of the project is well defined by the Product Breakdown Structure.

The First Scope Recommendation is to be generous in estimating the resources and time needed for inclusion in the brief, and must then make sure that the client understands that, due to the novel nature of projects, estimates of time and money for resources are based on 'best guesses'. This is simply due to the fact that each undertaking is unique and every individual venture will have its own set of unexpected problems. Some clients will press for a fixed cost project. If the commission is as relatively simple as, for instance, building a house – where materials can be calculated and costed – then this might be possible. But even here allowance should be written in to enable the builder to recover any major price increases of materials. It will also allow for other contingencies such as problems with foundations, water tables etc. It does not serve the client well if the builder ends up going bankrupt and walks off the job.

The Second Scope Recommendation is to communicate with the client. Project managers have to remember that they don't 'own' the project. They are providing a service on behalf of the client. When the terms of reference were first written it could well have been that the client had emphasised finishing on time as being crucial. However this does not give the project manager 'carte blanche' authority to spend extra money above budget in trying to make up for lost time whenever delays occur. Likewise if it becomes apparent that the specified completion date is under threat, the project manager has a duty to advise the client as early as possible.

The Third Scope Recommendation is to be meticulous in providing variation reports. If a client asks for a change – such as would it be possible to add, amend or whatever – and the project manager enthusiastically agrees, often these alterations are made and the project manager believes that the client has given a firm directive to go ahead. But eventually there is a day of reckoning and the client gets the bill. This will be a problem if when the client asked for the variation they did not realise that there would be an extra cost involved. For example at the early stage of house construction a request to move a window a metre to get a better view might not seem a big effort (after all the window exists and the house is still at the framework stage of construction), but this could well take the builder several hours of labour, for which he will charge. The culmination of several such minor changes, all at the request of the client (and perhaps even some suggested by the builder) might add up to several thousand pounds extra that had not been budgeted for by the client.

Turner (1999) explains the mechanics of scope management. He emphasises that its purpose is to ensure that adequate work is performed and that unnecessary effort is tackled. This means that the purpose of the job must be kept firmly in mind, and for every proposed action it has to be asked: is this really necessary for the achievement of the project? This practice helps to keep things on the task.

Stakeholder Management

Stakeholder management is the continuing development of a relationship with stakeholders for the purpose of achieving a successful project outcome (McElroy and Mills, 2000). A stakeholder can affect either the *project* scope or *product* scope. A stakeholder analysis therefore should be carried out at the very beginning of the project and must feed directly into the initial vision and scope document. A stakeholder analysis can uncover many useful aspects regarding the extent of the assignment, e.g. who has overlapping responsibilities and whose goals do not align with the responsibilities assigned to them; or which business processes are common and which are redundant. There are many ways of preparing this analysis. Some simple steps could be followed:

1. Determine who all the stakeholders are and categorise them according to their interest and influence in the project (see Figure 3.1).
2. Build awareness, influence, descriptions, goals and responsibilities for each.
3. Categorise each group of stakeholders, after preliminary interviews, according to their level of support for respective project goals. These categories could be 'strong support', 'passive support', 'neutral', 'passive opposition' and 'strong opposition'.
4. Identify both the current position and the required position.
5. Identify the reasons for opposition.
6. Develop an action plan (e.g. training, mentoring, change of responsibility, concession etc.) to bring each group of stakeholders to the required position.

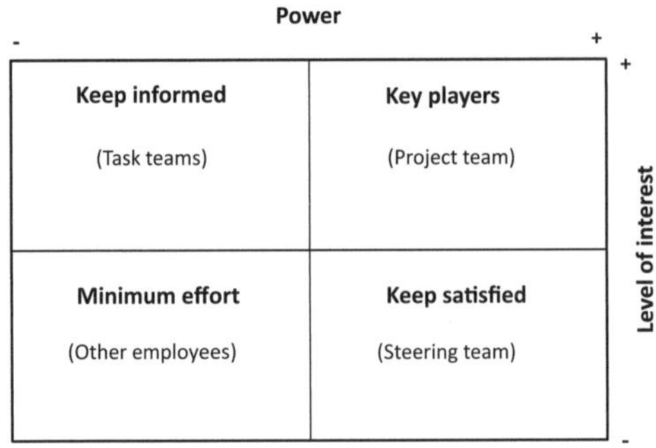

Power

Keep informed (Task teams)	**Key players** (Project team)
Minimum effort (Other employees)	**Keep satisfied** (Steering team)

Level of interest

Figure 3.1   Stakeholder matrix

You may use the matrix in Figure 3.1 as part of a group exercise not only to prioritise which stakeholders are the most important to consider but also to involve them in project design. A list of questions may be addressed to stakeholders:

- Who stands to lose or gain significantly from the project?
- Whose actions could potentially affect the project's success?
- Who has doubts about the goals and outcome of the project?
- Who is aware of the goals and confident of success?

Although it is vital to ensure stakeholder analysis at the earliest stage of the project, it is a dynamic process. The position and level of commitment of each group of stakeholders will change as their knowledge and engagement with the project will vary. Furthermore, new stakeholders may appear at subsequent phases of the undertaking. It is sensible to accept that you may not 'win them all', and it is often innovative to form a coalition of heterogeneous ideas. The primary focus should be on gaining the support of the 'key players' who control major resources and who have the highest influence on project outcomes.

Supply Chain Management Awareness

Blocking supply chain management's participation from the beginning typically leaves you with a hole in the budget. The crisis may occur during a construction or renovation project. One likely scenario is that with the building shell erected and nearly complete, along with the internal power and communication network around the skeletal framework, the project leaders contact supply chain management to start supplying and outfitting the rooms or campus with the necessary devices and equipment. Unfortunately, supply chain management, with capable support from procurement planners and equipment vendor representatives, learns that the lead time for importing a critical item of equipment from Japan is at least nine months. To compound the situation, they find that the doorways are too narrow for bringing the necessary equipment inside the building shell. This may be an extreme example; however it does illustrate the risk of embedding supply chain awareness at the very early stage of the project.

Supply Chain Managers logically will contend that they should be recruited to participate much earlier in the procurement and construction process. An eight-step approach is suggested that should spotlight supply chain management's relevant contributions and awareness at the more timely early phase of the project (Barlow, 2010):

1. Be organisationally curious and learn about impending or potential projects as early as possible.
2. Don't wait to be asked to join a project team. Ask for a seat at the table.
3. Contact peers or colleagues who have worked on successful projects and ask for advice or follow their example.
4. Research similar projects and document the lessons learned.
5. Provide the project team, including equipment planners, with supply chain information that can positively impact the project in terms of reducing the cost or preventing change orders.
6. Sell yourself and emphasise the potential benefits to having your wisdom available on the project team.
7. Point out your expertise on decisions that will have a long-term positive impact after the project is finished and the consultants have left.
8. Leverage your supply chain managers to see what sort of knowledge and skills they can provide to support your role on the project.

RESOURCES AND TIME MANAGEMENT

Resources and time management is the second of our six building blocks for project supply chain management. This element relates closely to project organisation and planning. The primary purpose of planning is to ensure that the necessary resources, both internal and external, are in place in order to produce specified deliverables on time and in budget. The second purpose of planning is to establish a set of directions in sufficient detail to steer the project team as to what must be done and when. From the standpoint of supply chain management there are three main parts involved in this building block:

- Supply chain organisation
- Developing a business case
- Resources and time scheduling.

Supply Chain Organisation

The purpose of project organisation is, 'to marshal adequate resources (human, material and financial), of an appropriate type to undertake the work of the project, so as to deliver its objectives successfully' (Turner, 1999, p. 124). Any elementary project management textbook covers the common bases and types of project organisation. At one end of the scale, the project is one part of the functional division of a company. This alternative to not giving the project a separate location or unit is usually applied to company-based smaller projects. This is also known as 'functional organisation'. At the other end of the spectrum occurs the case where the project is separated from the rest of the parent system as a self-contained unit. This is also called a 'line organisation'.

There are advantages and disadvantages to both of the above structures. In a functional organisation there is maximum flexibility in the use of staff and expertise but the client is not the focus of activity here. The project manager has full authority over a project in a line organisation. The need for technological knowledge is often passed to external consultants, depending on their availability. In an attempt to avoid the disadvantages of both functional and line organisations the 'matrix organisation' was developed as a combination of the two. A matrix organisation can take on a wide variety of forms, e.g. a coordinated matrix, secondment matrix and a balanced matrix.

In a coordinated matrix, a project controller is appointed with responsibility for coordinating tasks between functions, but with limited authority for ensuring priority is given for resources. By contrast in a secondment matrix the project manager has primary responsibility for resources, and assigns their work day by day. The operational managers second personnel, full or part-time, to the project as required and oversee the quality of the work that is carried out. Finally, in a balanced matrix a project manager is appointed to oversee the project and they share responsibility with the operational managers. The project manager is responsible for time and cost, the operational manager for scope and quality. Most of the major projects aim to follow a secondment matrix with ultimate responsibility to the project manager.

In the context of supply chain management the project manager must organise a contract between the parties involved, that is between the owner and contractor at the project level. In a major undertaking there should be dedicated resources for supply chain management in the matrix organisation to assist the project manager, as shown in Figure 3.2.

As illustrated in Figure 3.2, in addition to Team Leaders for key work packages, defined in the Work Breakdown, there should be functional managers to direct operations such as scope, quality, cost, time and risk across the project life cycle. A supply chain manager is also a functional supervisor, such as a Quality Manager.

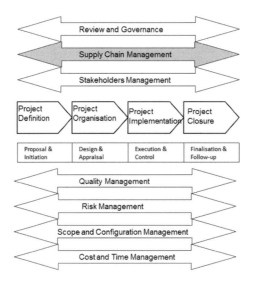

Figure 3.2   Supply chain management in project organisation

The specific responsibilities of a supply chain manager include managing the process of supplier selection, procurement process, and managing contracts. The supply chain manager is supported by team members to estimate forecast for sourcing requirements, keeping track of specifications, changes in suppliers, legal aspects and costs related to the contracts authorising the project. For a large project a supply chain manager and other functional leaders report directly to the project manager or through a Technical Manager (see Figure 3.3). The supply chain manager as part of a matrix organisation may also utilise experts from the parent organisation at exactly the right time of the project.

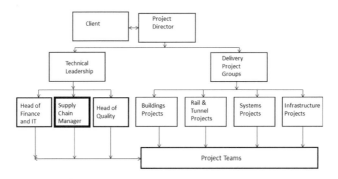

Figure 3.3   Supply chain management report line (reproduced with the kind permission of BAA)

In a line organisation the responsibility of each member is defined by his or her position in the hierarchy. However in a matrix organisation the accountability of each person is not clear. There are two forms of responsibility chart or tool that are used in a matrix organisation. The simpler version is RACI (**R**esponsible, **A**ccountable, **C**onsulted and **I**nformed) and a more complex edition is XDdPTCIA (e**X**ecutes the work, takes **D**ecision ultimately, takes **d**ecision jointly, manages work **P**rogress, provides **T**uition on the job, must be **C**onsulted, must be **I**nformed, available to **A**dvise). The responsibility chart should be simple and not used for passing the blame, and for that reason RACI is more commonly applied. Establishing the responsibility chart for supply chain management should involve all participants in the project and not just team members of supply chain management.

In some projects a supply chain manger may have an advisory role rather than a key functional role with the responsibility of procurement as shown in Figure 3.3. In this case the supply chain manager may report to the procurement administrator or the commercial director. In large global engineering, procurement and construction organisations (e.g. Fluor, Bechtel, Foster Wheeler) a corporate centre of excellence on supply chain management offers expertise in procurement and supply chain practices to major projects managed by them (see Figure 3.4).

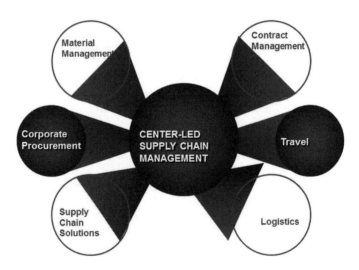

Figure 3.4   A corporate supply chain management organisation (reproduced with the kind permission of Fluor)

Developing a Business Case

A Business Case justifies the start-up of a project. It includes a description of the business problem or opportunity, the costs and benefits of each alternative solution; and the recommended resolution for approval. The business case is referred to frequently during the project to determine whether it is currently on track. Therefore it is vital that the supply chain requirements of a project should be embedded in the business case and also that concerted efforts and care are required to develop the business case for the project.

It is this business case, owned by the sponsor, that is the key document of the planning phase of the project life cycle. It provides a foundation for the feasibility of the range of options available to deliver project objectives. Table 3.1 shows the contents of a typical business case.

Table 3.1   The contents of a typical business case

Business Case: Contents
• Introduction and Executive Summary
• Business objectives and benefits
• Scope of the project
• Deliverables
• Timescales
• Quality and HSE plan
• Risks (Threats and Opportunities)
• Assumptions and constraints (PESTEL)
• Project strategy
• Options considered
• Supply considerations
• Costs and appraisal
• Project organisation
• Change control
• Information system and reporting

Business case development is a collaborative effort. It is business driven and led by the Sponsor and the programme area making the proposal. The key stakeholders who will be impacted by the proposal are consulted during the development of the document. The specialists for respective functions contribute to the relevant headings outlined in the contents above. For example, the quality manager prepares the quality and HSE plan, the accountant puts together costs and appraisal, the IT manager specifies information system and reporting etc. Likewise the supply chain manager is responsible for identifying supply considerations.

The section on supply considerations in the business case includes a description of the ability of the project team to supply materials, equipment, third-party skills and the facilities needed during the project. Existing supply conditions are important sources of information and the supply chain manager should assess the cost, quality, risks and availability of supply resources. Of particular interest will be an explanation of how control over contractors and subcontractors will be administered, and also how change orders will be handled.

Resources and Time Scheduling

Resources and time scheduling ranks high in the process of delivering the success of the Project Planning Chain. This scheduling is required to ensure that the resources working on the project are well coordinated and available. Likewise it is also critical that all activities of the scheme are delivered on time. There are two entities in the scheduling process, viz. allocating people resources and the arrangement of activities in a structured timeframe.

The starting point for both resource and time scheduling is the work breakdown structure (WBS) of the project. For each work package the activities and their estimated durations are identified. Resources are estimated by considering the trade-off between the resource requirement and the activity duration. For example, 120 man days can deliver an activity in 10 days by 12 men, in 12 days by 10 men or in 15 days by eight men. As the time parameters are first to be planned the scope for resource planning may already have been constrained. The next step is to forecast the total resource requirement by discipline or interchangeable skills. The forecast of resources is commonly presented for each work package in a bar chart supported by a histogram (as shown in Figure 3.5).

In practice, the forecasting of resources is not as simple as you may think. Certain contractors work in multiple trade gangs, e.g. a bricklayer, plasterer, electrician and pipe fitter may work together and some contractors may have to follow a demarcation of skills. Furthermore the efficiency of resources may vary. It is also useful to develop a forecast of all required resources by skills by aggregating the forecast of all work packages. The smoothing of resource allocation is also a favourable process in resource scheduling. Resources get assigned based on their skill and commitment.

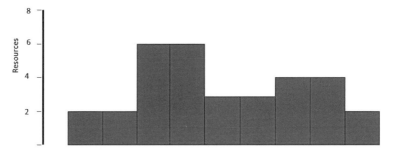

Activity	Week 1	Week 2	Week 3	Week 4	Week 5	Week 6	Week 7	Week 8	Week 9
A	2	2							
B			▪▪▪▪▪	▪▪▪▪▪	2	2			
C			6	6					
D					▪▪▪▪▪	▪▪▪▪▪	3	3	
E					1	1	1	1	
F									2
Total	2	2	6	6	3	3	4	4	2

Figure 3.5   An example of resource forecast in a bar chart

Both Microsoft Project (www.microsoft.com/project) and Oracle Primavera (www. oracle.com/us/primavera) include modules for resource scheduling. There are also specialist software systems, e.g. Innate (www.innate.co.uk), available in the market. As tasks and dates change, new requirements are highlighted and scenarios help to evaluate alternatives and reschedule resources. Therefore appropriate computer software is a useful aid in resource scheduling. It is generally accepted that a project team in a work package is likely to be more adaptable and motivated when they participate in the planning process.

When resources are overloaded and allocated with little float in the time schedule there are a number of options to augment the supplies available. These include working overtime, additional shifts, increased efficiency and deploying subcontractors. By contrast, resources may also be underutilised, and here too there are a number of options for reducing available reserves. These include moving resources to other activities, deploying them in maintenance, organising training and sending them on leave or even embarking on a process of laying-off. Clients often require a manpower plan to ensure that contractors have sufficient skills and labour to meet project objectives. Thus we can see that an acceptable forecast and schedule of resources is an important requirement of the planning chain of a major project.

In time scheduling, in addition to bar charts the best known tool is the Network Diagram, which is also known as the Critical Path Diagram. The work breakdown structure provides a carefully configured dissection of the project scope into manageable work packages. These can be further developed into activities. When the duration of each activity and the logical relationship between each action (precedence) are established, a network diagram may be defined as a graphical presentation of the project's activities. Table 3.2 shows a simple example of a project with 13 activities (A to M) and their precedence relationships and durations.

Table 3.2   An example of project activities for a network diagram

Activities	Depends on	Duration
A	-	2
B	A	4
C	A	2
D	C	10
E	B	3
F	E	3
G	F	4
H	E	2
I	H	2
J	G, I	3
K	D, J	2
L	B	2
M	K, L	1

The graphical presentation of network diagrams can take different shapes, e.g. 'activity on arrow', 'activity on node' or 'activity on box' forms of diagrams. The most common form is now 'activity on box' (as shown in Figure 3.6) since the introduction of 3M Post-it® Notes. Furthermore 'activity on box' diagrams have the advantage of showing the duration and float data for each activity on the box. As illustrated in Figure 3.7, the box contains the sections Earliest Start, Activity Duration, Earliest Finish, Activity Name, Latest Start, Total Float and Latest Finish.

Some of these terms are self-explanatory. *Earliest start* is the earliest date by which an activity can start and, likewise, *Earliest Finish* is the initial date by which an activity can be completed. Likewise, *Latest Start* is the final date an activity can commence and *Latest Finish* denotes the ultimate point when an activity can finish to meet the planned completion date. Both Earliest Start and Earliest Finish are determined by the 'forward pass' process, while the 'backward pass' method is applied to obtain the Latest Finish and Latest Start. *Total Float* is the difference between Latest Finish and Earliest Finish. It is a measure of flexibility or the inherent slack time in an activity's scheduling. The longest path with no float constitutes the critical path (e.g. path ABEFGJKM is the critical path in Figure 3.6). The activities on the critical path must be achieved at their earliest possible times in order to finish the project at its scheduled date.

Figure 3.6 offers a simple example of a network diagram in order to illustrate its characteristics. In a major project there are several work packages and a total network diagram becomes complex. Furthermore, a detailed analysis of a network diagram can be more complicated when the variable estimates of duration, 'float' or 'slack', resource levelling and the probability of occurrence are considered. Generally people also find network diagrams are difficult and time consuming to draw manually. Fortunately computer systems (e.g. MS Project and Oracle Primavera) are available to produce, schedule and maintain a network diagram and provide critical path analysis for effective time scheduling.

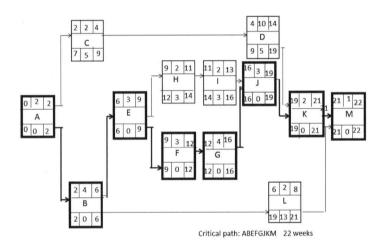

Critical path: ABEFGJKM   22 weeks

Figure 3.6   An example of a network diagram and floats

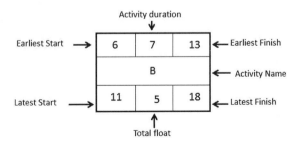

Figure 3.7   Basic notations of a network diagram

PROCUREMENT AND SUPPLIER FOCUS

Procurement and supplier focus is the third of our six building blocks for project supply chain management, and arguably this is the most focused building block of the entire project supply chain. The procurement or purchasing of goods and services from a multitude of suppliers has been the traditional home of supply chain management in projects. The roles and responsibilities for the supervision of procurement in a large project can be seen as a hierarchical sequence of authorisation between various levels of the project organisation from sponsor (or client) to subcontractor. These cascade down from the strategic and commercial drivers acting on the Sponsor and progress through various parties in the entire supply chain according to the procurement strategy and procurement process. This building block can be described in three components, such as procurement strategy, procurement process and procurement schedule.

Procurement Strategy

The first step of procurement planning is determination of the procurement strategy. Consideration is given to packages of work, types of contract or partnership with major contractors and the various tiers of subcontractors. Primary decisions will required in the procurement strategy regarding whether all of the project work should be procured from a single vendor or if a significant portion should be obtained from multiple vendors. Variations of procurement strategies do exist which are hybrids of the following strategies:

- Client-controlled strategy
- Turnkey strategy
- Joint ventures and partnering (contract partnership)
- In-house strategy.

As shown in Figure 3.8, the selection of procurement strategy depends on the levels of in-house manpower capacity and expertise in design, engineering and building. In-house strategy of the design, build and delivery may apply to relatively small or sensitive projects. In practice all major projects follow one or a combination of the other three procurement strategies.

The key player in a Client-controlled scheme (which is also the traditional procurement strategy in the construction industry) is the sponsor or client, consultants and contractors. A client initiates and authorises a project. A consultant undertakes the feasibility and design and a contractor is responsible for implementing the task. The client appoints a Project Board and a Project Director who selects consultants and the Main Contractor. The subcontractors are chosen by this main contractor. The Heathrow Terminal 5 project is an example of a client-controlled strategy which is commonly applied during the project planning chain or the pre-contract phase.

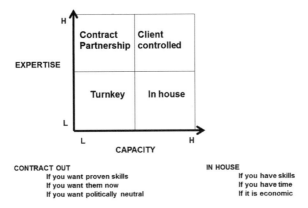

Figure 3.8   Procurement strategy

In a Turnkey strategy, the main contractor has the responsibility for the design, construction and commissioning phases of a project. Usually the client appoints a functional project manager who, along with his or her project team, prepares and monitors a performance specification and scope document. The turnkey contractor's project manager has executive authority and more multidisciplinary responsibilities to coordinate the project supply chain. The London Olympic 2012 project is broadly following a turnkey strategy and the Olympic Delivery Agency is the turnkey contractor. This strategy is preferred during the project delivery chain or the post-contract phase.

Primarily because of the financing sources of larger projects, joint ventures (JVs) or partnering strategies are emerging particularly for public sector projects. Local or regional government policies in some countries (e.g. China) prescribe joint venture procurement strategies. The Public-Private Partnership (PPP) is a hybrid of JVs in the UK government-sponsored projects where funding is sourced from both the public and private sectors. To operate within these PPP organisations the project manager is confronted by two types of diverse cultures and yet has to secure effective decisions in the project supply chain.

Case example: what is a public-private partnership?

Any collaboration between public bodies, such as local authorities or central government, and private companies tends to be referred to as a public-private partnership (PPP).

British Prime Minister Tony Blair is keen to expand the range of private public partnerships because he believes it is the best way to secure the improvements in public services that the Labour Government promised at the last election.

He believes private companies are often more efficient and better run than bureaucratic public bodies.

In trying to bring the public and private sector together, the government hopes that the management skills and financial acumen of the business community will create better value for money for taxpayers.

Many public sector unions, however, remain sceptical – and are particularly concerned about the extension of the private sector into new areas like schools and hospitals which have traditionally been publicly run.

Source: BBC News, 12 January 2003

The traditional Service Level Agreements (SLAs) where suppliers are penalised for non-conformance of time, cost and specifications are not appropriate for procurement strategy based on partnerships. The traditional procurement thinking should be revisited and there ought to be a move where a client organisation is actively managing the cause of risk or non-conformance and not the effect of that risk. The supply partners are in turn encouraged and incentivised to improve performance and create a competitive advantage for their businesses. This type of progressive partnership approach is illustrated by the so called 'T5 Agreement' of the London Heathrow Terminal 5 Project by the British Airport Authority (BAA).

In the UK construction industry the traditional roles and responsibilities of parties in executing a procurement strategy are as follows (Smith, 2000):

- A Client who initiates and sanctions a project.
- A Consultant who undertakes the feasibility of the design and identifies sourcing requirements.
- A Contractor who is responsible for implementing the project.

Case example: BAA T5 agreement

BAA's Terminal 5 programme at Heathrow Airport was one of Europe's largest construction projects, designed to cater for approximately 30 million passengers a year and to provide additional terminal and aircraft packing capacity. The facility opened to the public on 30 March 2008 and represented a £4.2 billion investment to BAA.

To achieve the audacious targets in money and programme that they had set themselves, BAA had to consider a novel contracting and procurement strategy. Suppliers signing up to BAA agreements were expected to work in integrated teams and to display the behaviours and values akin to partnering. Before embarking on the Terminal 5 (T5) programme of works BAA looked at a number of UK construction major projects to ascertain the lessons learnt, particularly where they had gone wrong. BAA decided that they had to have an agreement that could cope with an adaptable and dynamic approach, dealing with the uncertainties and embracing integrated teams. So BAA wrote their own bespoke agreement or contract. The same conditions of contract applied to all key suppliers, irrespective of type or usual position as a subcontract.

The key features of the T5 Agreement include:

- BAA as the client organisation held all the risk all of the time during the total life cycle of the project – on time, in budget and to quality.
- This was underpinned by BAA's unique insurance policy against risk. It was not so much about the cost of the BAA policy but the value it released. It did not increase the cost of the project as the insurance covered the supply chain on T5.
- As BAA would underpin all financial risks, thus contractors did not need to worry that they would be held financially accountable when things went wrong.
- Contractors or suppliers were committed to team work in partnership. There was requirement for a high level of transparency between BAA and their suppliers.
- Contractors worked to predetermined fixed profit levels.
- Profit was the key driver of supplier incentives. By taking away the financial risk BAA was removing the key commercial constraint, and thus suppliers were enabled to focus purely on technical delivery.
- The T5 Agreement was then supported by other documents such as the Commercial Policy which defined an appropriate commercial tension and the Delivery Agreement which was the legal deed and conditions of contract.

BAA divided the programme into 18 projects ranging in size from £10 million to £200 million. These were then split further into 150 sub-projects and then were divided into circa 1,000 work packages. The suppliers were engaged as and when on plans of work or where a supplier's capability was required. From the very start, BAA requested that suppliers work together in completing the projects, even those that are traditionally rivals or lower tier subcontractors. At a corporate level BAA ensured that all suppliers understood that corporate objectives were aligned to achieve a high-quality product within expected cost and enhance reputations. BAA also dealt with challenges in encouraging the entire workforce to understand, appreciate and trust the working relationship both between contractors and BAA. They constantly reinforced this message to the workforce.

The T5 project achieved completion, complying with targets for time, budget and quality and having generated a team working and partnership culture. The T5 Agreement as a whole looks to become a template in other major programmes. It now represents a serious alternative procurement route for major programmes of work and project supply chains.

Source: BAA Terminal 5 Project; Basu et al. (2009)

Procurement Process

The process of procurement, comprising methods and practices of procurement, differs for each individual client or contractor and for individual projects. The process will vary significantly according to whether the sponsor (client) or vendor (contractor) is the purchaser. For example, the sponsor will probably use a formal tendering process to invite bids, while a vendor may select second- or third-tier suppliers by negotiating with known providers of services or supplies. The procurement process will also be affected by the procurement strategy and the WBS as well as other project management processes. However there are many common sequences of components of the procurement process which may be customised depending on their ownership and application. These are shown below and illustrated in Figure 3.9 (Hamilton, 2004).

Pre-contract:

- Requisitioning of outsourced items
- Approving of vendors
- Issuing enquiries and tenders
- Evaluating vendor offers
- Awarding contracts and issuing purchase orders.

Post-contract:

- Preparing purchase schedules
- Expediting vendor orders
- Shop testing and acceptance
- Receipt and storage of supply items
- Closing out purchase orders.

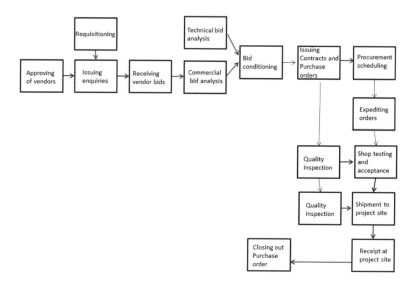

Figure 3.9   Procurement process

Requisitioning of outsourced items
From each work package of the WBS, the requirements of outsourced items (e.g. people, services, equipment, systems and materials) are prepared to meet the project delivery schedule. It is normal that such requirements are categorised by work packages and then grouped by possible vendors. A major undertaking requires a formal requisitioning process which should be approved by the Project Board before it may go to the next stage of issuing enquiries.

Approving of vendors
One of the critical challenges faced by supply chain managers is the selection of strategic partners who will furnish them with the necessary products, services, and materials in a timely and effective manner. Strategic supplier selection processes, underpinned by the procurement strategy of the project, require consideration of a number of factors beyond those used in operational decisions. There is an increased emphasis on manufacturing and organisational philosophies such as Just-

in-Time (JIT) and Six Sigma, as well as the growing importance of supply chain management concepts. Bearing these factors in mind, the need for considering supplier relationships from a strategic perspective has become even more apparent.

There are many approaches of selecting a strategic first-tier supplier. For example, using the framework based on the Analytical Network Process or ANP (Saaty 1996) a supplier could be evaluated and screened technically based on a number of factors. These include:

- Emphasis on quality at the source
- Design competency
- Process capability
- Experience delivering projects on schedule
- Legal suits and claims
- Hours of operator training in Total Quality Management (TQM)/Six Sigma
- Present workload
- Equipment/labour flexibility
- Dedicated allocation of resources
- Production and process innovation.

Other criteria such as the financial standing of the vendor and references from previous clients are included in the due diligence studies when the first tier suppliers or strategic vendors are shortlisted. After the list of approved suppliers is prepared it is important to establish a relationship with each supplier, provide a high level of attention and evaluate the relationship with continuous feedback.

The buying organisation or the client has the direct opportunity to select the first tier main contractor. Consequently the subsequent levels of contractors, subcontractors and suppliers are chosen by the respective contractors. The client usually exercises indirect influence in the selection of subcontractors. This process is illustrated in Figure 3.10.

Issuing enquiries and tenders
The preparing and issuing of enquiries or tenders will depend on whether the procurement comprises a major part or specific aspect of the project. For example the procurement of specialist advice can be obtained by developing a brief paper, which is commonly known as an 'invitation'. This document invites potential vendors to submit their proposals containing objectives, methodology, a timetable and fees to achieve the deliverables specified in the invitation briefing. However the procurement of the whole work package or the major part of the project is acquired by a more detailed process known as the 'tender documentation'. This documentation would include the form of tender, form of performance bond, form of agreement, specifications, drawings, bills of quantities and information of tenderers.

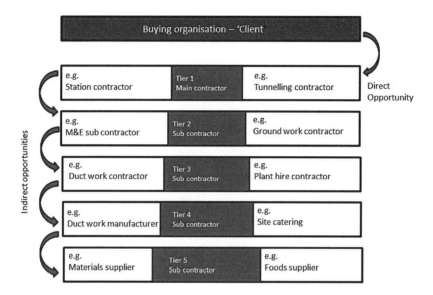

Figure 3.10   Selection of contractors and subcontractors (reproduced with the kind permission of Crossrail)

Within the European Union, tenders concerning all purchases over £25,000 should be followed in conjunction with the Procurement Procedure process flow of the *Official Journal of the European Union* (*OJEU*) (www.ojeu.eu).

Evaluating vendor offers

The evaluation of vendor offers usually consists of the receipt of vendor bids, commercial bid analysis, technical bid scrutiny and bid conditioning. The procurement team keeps a register of invitations made and bids received. Each offer is assessed both for its technical and commercial merits, usually by comparing scores for each evaluation criterion. 'Bid conditioning' is the term used for the subsequent modifications of the vendor offer following discussion or negotiation between the buyer and the vendor. At some stage the modified offer becomes the official offer.

Awarding contracts and issuing purchase orders

When the bid from a vendor is approved by the Project Board a contract is awarded to the vendor. The tender document becomes the contract document, bearing the signatures of both the buyer and the vendor. The project manager or the sponsor will also send a 'letter of appointment' to formalise the contract. The purchase order is then issued, usually in conformance with the *New Engineering Contract (NEC)* guidelines (NEC3, 2005).

The issuing of the purchase order concludes the 'pre-contract' practices of the procurement process. The procurement team will collect all documentation and purchase orders for the vendors that have been placed. The procurement team will update the procurement schedule developed during the definition and planning phases of the project by using information obtained from vendors.

Expediting of orders includes all activities aimed to ensure that the terms and conditions of the purchase orders and contracts are followed, with regular communication between the vendor and the project office. Expediting is also closely linked with inspecting during the fabrication or manufacture of the supply item. Planning for transportation and shipping requirements usually commences early in the supply process to minimise the lead time for delivery.

The project site office, which may be managed by the principal contractor, will have the responsibility of receiving, inspecting according to the quality standards and storing all equipment and supplies. The systems should ensure that current stocks do not create shortfalls and seek to avoid excess supplies. Stock management will be discussed in greater depth in Chapter 4. The closing out of purchase orders and contracts includes ensuring that the vendor has delivered what was contracted on time and at an acceptable quality standard. The payments are authorised usually according to the NEC guidelines (NEC3, 2005) influencing the terms and conditions in the contract.

It is important to note that contracts of high-risk deliverables should be formulated with legally binding agreements and managed with minimum changes. Other contracts carrying a lower level of risk should be managed with a non-adversarial approach of supplier partnerships.

The project schedule is discussed in the following section, and other procurement practices for the 'post-contract' period of the project delivery chain will be discussed further in the next chapter.

Procurement Schedule

The procurement schedule is a key piece of database used to monitor the progress of purchase orders and review them in conjunction with the construction schedule. The construction schedule for each work package is documented in bar charts and, where appropriate, is supported by a network diagram. The procurement schedule should be considered after reviewing the network diagram and bar chart of the construction schedule.

The procurement schedule for each work package is documented in a spreadsheet and a bar chart. Sometimes the schedule is also presented as a network diagram. A master procurement schedule at a high level of procurement contracts is developed and compared regularly with the master construction schedule. Table 3.3 shows a simple and hypothetical example of a master procurement schedule.

Table 3.3   An example of a master procurement schedule

Contract number	Description	Vendor	Work packages	Date of contract	Expected date of completion	Lead time
	Design	A	1, 2, 3, 4, 5	February 2009	March 2010	13 months
	Enabling works	B	8, 9, 10, 20	August 2009	December 2010	17 month
	Tunnels, portals and shafts	C	11, 12, 13, 14	December 2009	March 2013	52 months
	Stations	C	15, 16	March 2010	July 2012	29 months
	Systems	D	6, 7	June 2011	March 2014	34 months
	Logistics	B	21, 22, 23	March 2010	June 2011	16 months
	Rolling stocks and depots	C	17, 18, 19	December 2010	September 2013	34 months

It is emphasised that this example of a master procurement schedule is shown at a high level, but the more detailed schedule for each work package contains further items of information in the spreadsheet – including purchase order reference, category of work, actual start date of contract, total value of the order, value per annum and responsibility.

The master procurement schedule is also supported by a bar chart as shown in Figure 3.11. If any construction activities are delayed due to late procurement, the network diagram of the total project is reviewed to see if the knock-on effect delays any other activities. It is important to identify the procurement items which have a long lead time, especially if they are on the critical path, and also to identify any special logistics requirements.

SUMMARY

In this chapter we have explained the role and importance of the three building blocks in the Project Planning Chain. The purpose of planning is to ensure and facilitate the future outcomes of a project. However as a Japanese proverb says, 'A plan without actions is a day dream.' Thus project supply chain planning in each building block is supported by appropriate actions to take advantage of the synergy of the supply chain practices in major schemes. The roles and responsibilities of key stake holders in each building block are also explained: e.g. the part played by the sponsor or client or customer, consultant, contractor/subcontractor/supplier and supply chain manager. Procurement and supplier focus is arguably the most critical building block. It is recognised that having established the scope and methodology of the project, its success is critically balanced by the procurement strategy, the procurement process and partnership with major contractors and suppliers

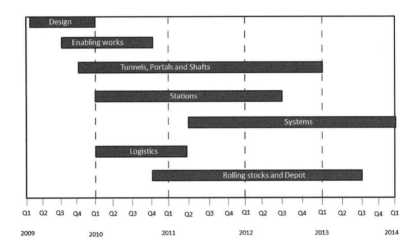

Figure 3.11   A master procurement schedule bar chart (reproduced with the kind permission of Crossrail)

CHAPTER 4

PROJECT DELIVERY CHAIN

INTRODUCTION

The outcome of the Project Planning Chain is the awarding of contracts. It is at this phase that the Project Delivery Chain begins. The importance of meeting all project commitments on time, within budget and at acceptable quality standards is reflected in the governance and management of the project delivery chain. This is ensured by the three building blocks of the project planning chain (see Figure 2.1), viz:

1. Supply management
2. Building and installation
3. Handover and closure.

If the project *planning* chain is managed by the Client (or Sponsor or Customer) with assistance from Contractors (or Consultants or Suppliers) then the project *delivery* chain is managed by contractors and suppliers with the support of the client. The delivery chain covers the Implementation and Closure phases of the project life cycle and also ensures the post-contract commitments of the procurement processes (see Chapter 3).

This chapter describes the key activities and processes under the three building blocks of the project delivery chain.

SUPPLY MANAGEMENT

When the contract has been awarded the primary requirement is to ensure the supply of organisation and people, facilities, equipment and materials. The Project Manager, who was appointed as part of the contract, usually calls for a 'kick-off' meeting to initiate the establishment of project organisation and support facilities. If the supply of resources and facilities is not ensured right at the beginning of the delivery chain, then the implementation processes and activities cannot be executed. There are many obvious requirements for building a project organisation; however, the following three supply prerequisites must be well managed to ensure the successful delivery of a major project:

1. Supply of organisation and people management
2. Supply of facilities management
3. Supply of equipment and materials management.

Supply of Organisation and People Management

The delivery chain of a major project is usually managed by a consortium of 'first tier' major contractors and occasionally led by a chief contractor for a 'turnkey' type of project. For example in the High Speed 1 (HS1) project for the construction of the Channel Tunnel Rail Link (CTLR), Rail Link Engineering (RLE) was appointed as Project Manager. RLE was actually a consortium of construction companies formed between Arup, Bechtel, Halcrow and Systra. Union Railways (UR) was allocated the responsibility to act as the client or sponsor of the project.

It is important to note that although the consortium of contractors is responsible for the execution of the project, the client is also involved in the delivery chain to ensure the project scope, as well as acting as a conduit to external stakeholders. When the London and Continental Railway (LCR) was awarded the concession to build the Channel Tunnel Rail Link, the UK Parliament provided the framework for the project in December 1996. As indicated earlier, the core organisation structure (see Figure 4.1) is underpinned by the client and project manager relationship and roles. LCR allocated the responsibility to UR to act as a client for the CTRL project. UR then appointed RLE as the project manager of CTRL. The two entities, UR and RLE, worked in partnership to deliver the project.

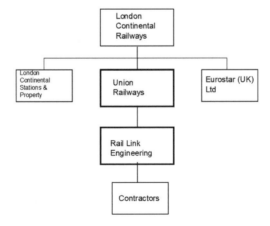

Figure 4.1   HS1 project organisation

UR, as the client, provided the interface with the key stakeholders who were the parties affected by the CTRL. These included the government, planning authorities, statutory environmental agencies, highway authorities and, ultimately, the operators (Eurostar and Network Rail). RLE constituted the interface with contractors and suppliers.

The benefits of the organisation of the project team as a matrix system is described in detail in many project management books (e.g. Turner, 1999) and also discussed in Chapter 3 here. However there is key success factor of the project delivery organisation that we can distil and learn from. This is the underlying philosophy in the contracts and agreements between the client and first tier contractors and also between the first tier contractors and other providers in the supply chain. The New Engineering Contract (NEC3, 2005) guidelines appear to encourage the flexibility of partnership between the client and contractors as stated below:

It is designed to be as flexible as possible. It can be used

– for engineering and construction work containing any or all of the traditional disciplines such as civil, electrical, mechanical and building work,

– whether the Contractor has full design responsibility, some design responsibility or no design responsibility,

– to provide all the current options for types of contract such as competitive tender (where the Contractor is committed to his offered prices), target contracts, cost reimbursable contracts and management contracts.

The Latham Report quoted in the NEC guidelines recommends that 'the industry and its customers use partnering' and also outlines 'Trusting the Team and the Seven Pillars of Partnering'. These 'seven pillars of partnering' in the NEC describe the second generation of collaboration and cooperation, which achieves even greater benefits. This is accomplished by adding a longer-term strategy to a series of projects undertaken by a single customer. It can be argued that the success of the T5 Agreement (see Chapter 3) is assisted by the fact that BAA has the capacity of engaging a group of approved contractors for a number of schemes.

However following the environmental problems of the oil spill in the Mexican Gulf in the summer of 2010 (*The Guardian*, 29 October 2010) current thinking on the supplier engagement process is shifting more towards legally explicit Service Level Agreements and contracts. There should be a correct balance as far as possible between the legally binding critical deliverables and the sharing of both risks and benefits between the client and contractors.

The supply of people management is also enhanced by the appropriate selection of skills in the internal organisation and the choice of the progressive tiers of suppliers. The importance of team building (Tuckman, 1965), continuous training and communication has been emphasised in many publications (Keegan et al. 2008; Tabassi and Bakar, 2009). The benefits of managing internal stakeholders are also discussed in Chapter 3. However it is also argued (Herman and Renz, 2002) that a 'silo culture' can be harnessed to the advantage of the focused and rapid delivery of a building work package. It is essential to note that during the closure stage of the project it is of paramount importance to have a phase of operation and training before handing over to the Client and the users of the outcome.

Supply of Facilities Management

The supply of facilities relates to project management offices, the support infrastructure and the logistics necessary to deliver project plans from physical locations. Paying attention to facilities is often the neglected item in project management practices, probably because it is often considered to be too obvious to afford this stage any serious consideration.

The project office provides a physical location for the project identity and the forum of project excellence. This is where project management systems are located and the operation plans, reporting and their maintenance are developed. The location of project offices is often determined by the availability of facilities and the position of construction sites. This is reflected in the following forms or in a hybrid state:

- The offices are geographically separated.
- Project task groups work in their own environment.
- Project task groups are co-located.

The formation of project offices is often the outcome of the close-out reports of similar undertakings which have identified project delivery problems associated with information delays, poor communication and cost overrun. The formation of project offices is also seen as a means to inculcate a common culture into the organisation, particularly towards enhancing a partnership between client teams and suppliers.

Projects are managed by communication and should be properly equipped with facilities for meetings and also the ICT infrastructure. The project offices should also provide a high-quality and comfortable working environment supported by good utilities and catering facilities. The logistics of moving team members between offices and construction sites should also be optimised. With the growing power of the Internet, the advantages of the virtual office should also be proportionately utilised.

Supply of Equipment and Materials Management

A study by McKenna and Wilczynski (2005) showed that capital projects in the USA topped $500 billion annually. This figure included 33 per cent as the cost of engineering equipment and building materials. The authors also claimed that up to 80 per cent of inventory levels were driven by poor attention to the forecasting of demand or the proliferation of the design. Although inventory management is a focused function in operation administration, it tends to constitute merely a 'Cinderella' level process in major schemes. Most of the projects are left with 'surplus' materials and equipment which are written off in accounting terms.

After the termination of projects it has become almost standard practice to expect surplus consumable and building materials to be either disposed of as waste or handed over as 'free issues' to the client. This acceptance is reflected in the inclusion of 'novation' in the NEC guidelines (NEC3, 2005). Novation is the procedure of transferring the contract of a supplier employed by the client to another contractor, or back to the client. In practice this usually applies to a designer in a design and build arrangement and the transfer of surplus stocks. The aim of this process is to shift responsibility from client to contractor or vice versa. The NEC does not expressly provide for novation as this system does not follow the principles of good management practice. The NEC considers that the end product of novation is effectively no different from the contractor entering into a contract with the new client from the outset. Therefore, a key objective of the Supply Chain Manager should be to minimise the causes of surplus stocks and also of novation by optimising the supply of engineering equipment and building materials.

The supply of engineering equipment and building materials should be provided with secured and easy-to-access warehousing and storage facilities at project sites. Heavy items of engineering equipment (e.g. compactors, excavators, dozers, loaders, forklift trucks and tunnelling equipment) are procured by contract hire and should have asset codes for easy identification. Building materials and consumables should be coded with reference to categories, location and work packages and recorded with information on suppliers, specifications, costs, stock levels and order quantities.

Inventory management is a good indicator of the effectiveness of supply chain management. It is relatively easy to achieve higher levels of customer service by accumulating excessive stocks. It will also obscure short-term operational problems. However this is a costly and risky option in terms of cash flow. Obsolete inventory – be it due to changes in technology, fashion, or in foodstuffs past their use-by date – has little salvage value. Thus it is vital to optimise the inventory level. With adequate warehousing and storage facilities, stocks are kept as a buffer along the supply chain in various project sites. These inventories can cost between a minimum of 15 per cent up to 40 per cent of their value per year (for instance, storage space, handling costs, energy outlay, including heating and refrigeration, stock slippage and insurance).

It is clear that careful management of stock levels makes good business sense. Safety stock is the buffer inventory to cover the variation in demand and supply during lead time. There are many uncertainties involved in demand and supply, which is an inexact science. For example, customers may increase an order, machinery might break down or a supplier might be unable to deliver on time due to transport problems. There are key parameters affecting the calculation of safety stock:

- Forecast accuracy
- Lead time
- Expected service level.

In traditional stock management there are two basic approaches: the 'pull' approach and the 'push' approach. In a pull system (Figure 4.2) a warehouse is viewed as independent of the supply chain and inventory is replenished with order sizes based on a predetermined stock level for each warehouse. By contrast, the stock management model for the pull system is normally geared to establish re-order level (ROL) and re-order quantity (ROQ). That is, when the stock drops to a certain level, a re-order of a predetermined amount is triggered. The re-order quantity takes into account past demands and the lead times for the re-order to be satisfied. The aim is to have as small an amount of inventory as possible on hand at any one time, and the re-order quantity should likewise be as small as possible.

However in some processes, such as a batch system, there will be a minimum amount that can be produced; and in other cases there can be economies of scale which will determine the optimal size of an order. The push method is used when economies of scale in procurement outweigh the benefits of minimum inventory levels as achieved in the pull method (Figure 4.3). In other words, the warehouse does not decide the quantity of the order but will receive a delivery as determined

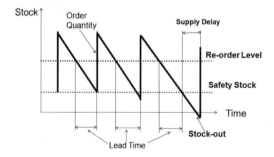

Figure 4.2   An ROL/ROQ 'pull' system

by the production schedule. Normally a fixed interval review model with a forecast demand for manufacturing planning is used in a push system.

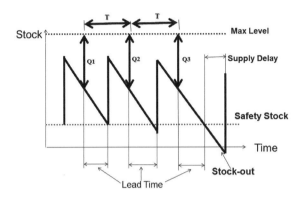

Figure 4.3   A fixed interval 'push' system

BUILDING AND INSTALLATION

In the Building and Installation (or Production) phase, heavy items of equipment are procured and civil work is undertaken. On completion of this civil work mechanical, electrical and control facilities are installed. This stage differs dramatically from the previous planning and procurement periods. First, whereas the previous segments are evolutionary in character, the Production element is highly mechanistic (Morris, 1973). The aim is not to develop new technical options but to build as efficiently as possible. Second, there is a large expansion in organisation.

At a construction site a management team is established to execute and control work physically in the arena. It is a proven practice to delegate the post-contract building and installation action activities to a major contractor or a consortium of contractors. Organisational responsibilities, control systems and communication processes can have a marked effect on the degree of day-to-day control of the project. There are many publications (Turner, 1999; Meredith and Mantel, 2003) explaining the requirements of the major activities and processes involved in the building and installation phase. These obligations include:

- Kick-off and launch
- Preparing Project Management Plans
- Organising facilities and resources
- Building a team

- Controlling requirements
- Celebrating key milestones.

The purpose of this book is primarily to focus on the role of supply chain management in major projects rather than elaborating on all the activities and processes in the project life cycle. However it is important to highlight also the role of 'project personality' in the production phase of the project. Nichols and Jones (2010) identified two types of 'project personality'. One is the 'silo' personality focusing internally on one element or function of the project. The other is a 'system' character thinking holistically of the project outcome. The authors argued that this 'silo' persona is most appropriate for the production phase, while holistic thinking and interfunctional team work are better suited to all other stages.

The specific role of supply chain management during building and installation include the supply of resources, equipment and materials underpinned by an effective logistics support and contractual or partnering agreement. It also important to ensure robust forecasting and review processes.

HANDOVER AND CLOSURE

The final stage of the project life cycle is the handover and closure of the project. Very often the success and sustainability of the outcome of a project is determined by how the final stage is dealt with. The administration of the Heathrow Terminal 5 project demonstrated some outstanding project management practices, including the quality and performance management system and the T5 Agreement of supplier partnership. However it can be argued that the end game of T5 created some public outcry. We all recall the newspaper articles at the time: 'Thousands of suitcases are being sent to Milan by British Airways to try to help clear a backlog of 19,000 bags at Heathrow's new Terminal 5' (*The Guardian*, 2 April 2008). The conclusions of the House of Commons Transport Select Committee Report (2008) highlighted that insufficient communication between the owner of the new terminal, BAA, and its operator, British Airways, was a major factor in the ensuing complications with the baggage system and security searches.

It may be easy to complete the work within the constraints, and think that constitutes a successful project. However failing to use the facility delivered to obtain the expected benefits may obfuscate all the credits of the earlier phases of the project life cycle. Therefore the handover and closure of a project deserves careful and high-priority attention in the project supply chain.

In the PRINCE2 (2009) guidelines there are three subprocesses relevant to this stage: CP1 (decommissioning a project), CP2 (identifying follow-on actions) and

CP3 (evaluating a project closure). Meredith and Mantel (2003) also suggest four ways of closing or terminating a project as summarised below:

- By Addition: in-house projects embedded in the business – sign of success.
- By Integration: major projects are operationalised – sign of success.
- By Starvation: slow demise by depleting budge – sign of failure.
- By Extinction: sudden demise by failure – sign of failure.

The key steps of project handover and closure as outlined by Turner (1999) appear to cover a comprehensive plan. These steps are:

- Finish the work
- Transfer the product to the user
- Obtain benefits
- Disband the team
- Review the progress.

In order to finish the work the team must ensure all work is completed in a timely and efficient manner. The following checklist should help the process.

- 'Snagging' or 'punch' lists
- Disposal of surplus materials
- Handover and commissioning teams
- Training the users
- Acceptance certificates
- Service agreements.

The skills required to finish a project are usually quite different from those required to start it up and run it. It is important to promote a high degree of interface with the users supported by appropriate training. Therefore it may be apposite to change the team in the final stage and also to retain a small group to see through the 'snag list'.

The key issues related to the reassignment of the product should include a plan for transfer, training the user in the operation of the facility and ensuring that the user formally accepts the product. It is good practice to follow a 'build-operate-transfer' (BOT) methodology. The signed acceptance certificate should result in a definite shift of responsibility, and the purchase order is closed with the final payment.

The realisation of expected benefits may take a longer period after the handover of the scheme. However a project audit should determine the potential benefits and assess the success criteria included in the business case.

This phase can bring its own difficulties. As Turner (1999) astutely observes, 'It is very easy for the good effort of execution and control to be lost, as some team members look forward to the next project, and others become demob happy or demob unhappy' (p. 328). It is important that the disbanding of the team is carried out in a planned manner with the full support of the Human Resources Department, providing as far as possible future placements and counselling for project team members. It is common to organise an 'end of project' party where well-deserved rewards and recognitions are conferred on members.

Finally, the project closure should be followed by a 'health check' or project audit (Wateridge, 2002) to identify the success factors, determine what went well and what could have been done better as valuable learning points for future projects.

The specific role of supply chain management at the handover and closure stage is to ensure that all warranties and maintenance contracts of facilities and the supply of spare parts are in place, and also that the purchase orders are closed and payments are made to all suppliers.

SUMMARY

In this chapter we have explained the role and importance of three building blocks in the project delivery chain. The role and the visibility of Supply Chain and Procurement Managers are arguably less prominent in the production phase of the project than at the planning stage. However, as is emphasised in this chapter, the issues related to the project chain should be continuously resolved during the project delivery chain. The critical factors include the forecasting of demand, stock management and logistics support to ensure that resources and materials are available on time, and the close-out of all purchase orders.

Finally, contractors and suppliers are key players in delivering the building and installation activities of a major project. Developing and sustaining contractor and supplier relationships across major projects is critical to the production phase of the project delivery chain. Contractors are more likely to share greater risks when clients develop a trusted relationship with them that encompasses a number of major projects.

CHAPTER 5

SUPPLY CHAIN INTEGRATION: SYSTEMS AND PROCEDURES

INTRODUCTION

We have described the components of the Project Supply Chain building blocks in Chapters 2 to 4, highlighting the major issues, opportunities and challenges inherent in managing a total supply chain. Now the key question is: how are these building blocks interfaced or integrated to provide the synergy for managing a total supply chain as one unit in a major project? The processes in each building block are standardised or formalised by systems and procedures of quality management and information management. The effectiveness of such systems and procedures can be achieved by using effective review and performance management processes.

There are three cornerstones for integrating the building blocks of both the planning and delivery phases of a project supply chain. These are:

1. Systems and procedures
2. Quality and performance management
3. Regular reviews

In this chapter the requirements, processes and deliverables of 'systems and procedures' are discussed

Systems and procedures in project management are guidelines for project governance. In a wider sense, project governance covers influencing and conducting the affairs of the project organisation in order to meet both the project objectives and ethics of social responsibility. It is true that there is an abundance of processing guidelines and regulatory policies designed to influence systems and procedures in a major project. However as indicated in Chapter 2, there are just three major categories of systems and procedures in the context of project supply chain:

*   External regulatory and internal quality standards
*   Financial and accounting procedures
*   Information and communication technology.

EXTERNAL REGULATORY AND INTERNAL QUALITY STANDARDS

External regulatory standards are mainly focused on health, safety and environmentally (HSE) related requirements. Acceptable standards of occupational health, safety and environment standards in major projects are achieved by a positive planned approach to all project activities. This should be supported by the appropriate training of both team members and suppliers. In order to maintain consistently high HSE levels, a formal and well-established health, safety and environment management system (HSEMS) is required. This process is developed by qualified project team members who possess the relevant knowledge and experience regarding recent legislation. Here are some specific examples of these requirements in current legislation:

- Design and Management Regulations 1994 (for tender and construction phase safety)
- The Railway Safety Regulations 1999
- International Environment Standards ISO 14000
- Environmental Permitting Regulation 2010
- Building Regulations 2010
- Control of Major Accident Hazards (COMAH) Regulations 1994.

Such regulatory guidelines are usually very detailed and often depend on their interpretation and application. The HSE guidelines for a major project should be derived from these legislations and address the key question: can the project be delivered without an unacceptable degree of risk to the HSE requirements to anyone working in this project or the facilities affected by them?

The HSE objectives of a major project are to ensure that – as far as is reasonably possible – it is safe for the stakeholders and free from risks to their health during the planning and delivery chains of the project supply chain. It is important to note that regular training and audits of HSE standards not only ensure these requirements but also act as galvanising factors between different supply chain building blocks and between client and suppliers. In an age when the spotlight is on environmental sustainability and climate change, it is inevitable that HSE guidelines in a major project should conform to such ecological requirements in a proportionate way. Since environmental sustainability and climate change are broad disciplines covering science, technology and social responsibility, the hope of doing justice to such a huge topic is considered beyond the scope of this book. However HSE guidelines should not reflect any denial of this aim of environmental sustainability.

The guidelines of quality standards of project management which are in the public domain comprise the *Body of Knowledge* (APM, 2006), the *Project Management*

Body of Knowledge: PMBOK (PMI, 2008), ISO 10006 (2003), PRINCE2 (2009) and BS 6079 (BSI, 2002).

The *Body of Knowledge* (BOK) tells us that 'quality applies to everything in project management: commercial, organisation, people, control, technical, etc.' That's fine, but just what is quality? BOK however recognises the dimension of Total Quality Management (TQM) as 'what the client really wants, defining the organisation's mission, measuring throughout the whole process how well performance meets the required standards'. The dimension of TQM involving the total organisation in the implementation of continuous improvement in a project environment was first described in Levitt and Nann (1994), and the BOK seems to have a passing reference to TQM.

In the PMBOK the definition of project quality is also unclear, although Section 8 of the document is dedicated to Project Quality Management comprising Quality Planning, Quality Assurance and Quality Control. However in Section 8.1, the paper identifies which quality standards are relevant to the project and determines how to satisfy them. It describes how the project management team will implement its quality policy with the aid of a formal quality plan. Quality seems to relate to 'standards'. These yardsticks are then put into the quality plan with a process that can identify whether or not the team is managing the project in accordance with the quality policy that has been established.

ISO 10006: Quality Management Systems – Guidelines for Quality Management in Projects claims to provide 'guidance on quality system elements, concepts and practices for which the implementation is important to, and has an impact on, the achievement of quality in project management'. However, the application of this document is more likely to have the opposite effect. If attention is given to all the items identified in the standards, the result could very well be a poorly managed and unnecessarily costly project that merely 'ticked all boxes' required in the standard. In fact, it identifies virtually the same set of project management processes and knowledge areas as PMBOK. There is no definition of quality and there is not even a quality management process.

By failing to include the quality management processes, ISO 10006 implies that these critical procedures lie outside the scope of project management. But how does one ensure quality without quality management? ISO 10006 merely identifies the quality plan as a document describing which general procedures and associated resources should be applied, by whom and when, to a specific project, product, process or contract. The standard recognises that project phases and project life cycles exist, but it provides no guidance on how the identified project processes relate to project phases. Pharro (2002) comments, 'The guide [ISO 10006)] focuses on the standard of project management and does not cover the *doing* of the activities necessary to complete the project' (p. 109).

PRINCE2 (2009) is a project management methodology owned and maintained by the UK government. PRINCE2 is a government standard that has grown organically to be adopted by both private and public organisations. The document identifies 'quality in a project environment' as a PRINCE2 component and 'quality review technique' as a PRINCE2 technique. This methodology presumes that the project will be managed under the umbrella of a published Quality Management System (QMS) conforming to ISO 9001. QMS in PRINCE2 appears to be similar to a quality plan indicated in ISO 10006 and PMBOK. There is no clear definition of quality in the document and the link between 'quality in a project environment' and the 'quality review technique' is also unclear. However, the guidelines for the formal quality review in a project are useful and comprise three steps:

1. Preparation: where the project deliverable or product is measured against quality criteria contained in the product description, and question lists are created.
2. Review: where the product is 'walked through' against question lists and follow-up actions are agreed.
3. Follow-up: where the identified errors in the product are fixed, agreed and signed off.

BS 6079 (BSI, 2002) is a *Guide to Project Management*. The document identifies the key stages of the project life cycle and the project management processes are divided into two parts, namely Project Planning and Project Control. It appears to be most suitable for large engineering projects with the project manager being in full control. It is not prescriptive regarding project management techniques and there is no clear definition of quality in BS 6079. A definition of quality is also missing in *BS 6079 Part 2: Vocabulary* (2000). As regards the quality plan, the document refers to ISO 10006 and thus suffers from similar weaknesses in the area of quality management.

FINANCIAL AND ACCOUNTING PROCEDURES

Traditionally accountants have seen themselves as the major channel through which quantitative information flows to management. Accountants work on historical data regarding what has happened, and their reports cover arbitrarily set periods of time, with little allowance that business activities do not stop on 30 June or 31 December (or whatever other date has been designated as the time to take a snapshot of the financial position of the business). From a conventional point of view, and from the standpoint of stakeholders such as shareholders and bank managers, there has to be a way of measuring the performance of an organisation and currently there is no better method than accounting reports. It follows, therefore, that for accountants to do their job of reporting to meet conventional requirements, information will be required from the operational arm of the business. This cannot be disputed. Therefore if information is being provided, then it is useful to try to use that data to improve the productivity of the organisation.

In response to pressures from stakeholders there is a risk of overemphasis on short-term financial performance. Consequently this myopic approach results in overinvestment in short-term fixers and underinvestment in longer-term development plans. Furthermore, the emphasis on short-term results can cause organisations to reduce costs in general across the board target without any effective analysis of value-creating activities.

It makes sense therefore that financial factors are integrated with work packages and that project managers and team members can focus on the cost advantage of procurement and project deliverables. Improved quality, delivery and flexibility should eventually develop the profit margin, but the impact of any items of project cost is straight to the accountants' 'bottom line'. There are indications that there has been a gradual shift in project management towards financial administration, probably influenced by the following factors:

- The growth of the 'share owning' population has generated a new breed of consumers who are interested in the financial performance of a company. This has required financial management to become conscious of external requirements.
- With the increase in external sourcing and third-party operations, the cost base and its control in manufacturing and services have been sharpened.
- The economic recession in the late 1980s, early 1990s and the comprehensive spending reviews in 2010 in the UK forced many manufacturing and service industries to adopt restructuring and cost-reduction initiatives. Project managers are also tightening their project spends.
- Finally, in the well-publicised Balanced Scorecard the role of the financial outlook, as one of the four perspectives, has been accepted by operations mangers since 'financial measures are valuable in summarising the readily measurable economic consequences of actions already taken' (Kaplan and Norton, 1996, p. 22).

It is therefore important for any major project to focus on the key issues of financial management in order to enhance competitiveness through operations cost advantages. These issues include achieving project objectives, understanding strategic cost factors and cost effectiveness.

Achieving Financial Objectives

We do not intend to delve into the sophisticated world of financial management involving the methods of financing, tax implications, currency movements etc. However, as indicated earlier, it is important that key financial parameters and objectives of the business should be understood and incorporated in manufacturing objectives. These key financial concepts are:

- *Sales value*: the total turnover of the business in money terms.
- *Net profit*: the money made by the business after charging out all costs. This can be expressed before tax or after tax.
- *Capital employed*: total investment tied up in the business comprising shareholders funds. With the double entry system of accounting, shareholders' funds, or capital, will always equal the total of all the assets, less all the liabilities.
- *Working capital*: working capital refers to the funds available, and is the difference between current assets (debtors, inventory, bank balances and cash) and current liabilities (creditors, short-term loans and the current portion of long-term loans).
- *Cash flow*: cash-flow statements show where and how the working capital has increased or decreased.

The above concepts of financial objectives in project management are borrowed from operations management. The more specific financial objectives of a project start with the feasibility of the project by analysing the options with key financial indicators, such as net present value (NPV) and internal rate of return (IRR). This is followed through in the procurement of strategy, selection of suppliers and delivering each work package of the project on budget. An important tool to manage cost and time schedules according to the delivered value of each work package is Earned Value Management (EVM).

Earned Value Management

Earned value management or Earned Value Analysis is a project control tool for comparing the achieved value of work in progress against the project schedule and budget. It can be performed at a single activity level and by aggregating the results up through the hierarchy or work breakdown structure. There are a few useful terms related to earned value management as defined below:

- *Time Now*: the reference point used to measure and evaluate the current status.
- *Earned Value*: the value of useful work done at Time Now. It is also known as the Budgeted Cost of Work Performed (BCWP). It is typically calculated at activity level by multiplying the Budget at Completion for the activity with the percentage progress achieved for that activity.
- *Budget at Completion*: the total budget for the work to be carried out.
- *Original Duration*: the planned overall duration of the activity or project.
- *Planned Value (Spend)*: the planned rate of spend against time though the life of the project. It is also known as the Budget Cost of Work Schedule (BCWS).

- *Actual Cost*: the cumulative costs incurred at Time Now. This is also known as the Actual Cost of Work Performed (ACWP).
- *Cost Variance (CV)*: the difference between the Earned Value and the Actual Cost at Time Now (CV = Earned Value – Actual Cost).
- *Scheduled Variance (SV)*: the difference between the Earned Value and the Planned Value at Time Now (SV = Earned Value – Planned Value).
- *Scheduled Performance Index (SPI)*: the ratio between the Earned Value and Planned Value at Time Now (SPI = Earned Value/Planned Value). It is used to predict the final outcome of the project time, i.e. the estimated time of completion (ETC).
- *ETC*: planned completion time/SPI.
- *Cost Performance Index (CPI)*: the ratio between the Earned Value and Actual Cost at Time Now (CPI = Earned Value/Actual Cost). It is used to forecast the Estimated Cost at Completion (EAC).
- *EAC*: budget Cost/CPI.

Earned value management has been applied effectively in well-structured projects, especially engineering projects, where there is a defined work breakdown structure and various levels of hierarchy. It is not a progress control tool in itself, as it can only highlight a need for corrective action by indicating trends. At each milestone review (i.e. Time Now), it provides some useful pointers of project control including:

- *Variance analysis*: it shows the current status in terms of cost and schedule.
- *Estimating accuracy*: it enables predictions of cost at completion and completion date.
- *Efficiency*: it provides performance indices identifying areas requiring corrective action.

However, there is a danger in placing too much reliance on earned value management because the results are likely to be flawed for a number of reasons. These include:

- Forecasts depend on reliable measurements of the amount of work performed and this can be difficult to achieve in some cost types.
- A considerable amount of clerical effort is needed to maintain the database and carry out calculations.
- Difficulty is likely to be greatest for projects containing a higher proportion of procured equipment and materials.
- It does not take into account risks and uncertainties.
- If the methodology of EVM is not fully understood by the sponsor and members of the project, it becomes difficult to get everyone's cooperation.

The principles of EVM are conceptually simple but detail rich. In the above example, we have looked at only one activity; but the earned value and its related parameters would have to include all project work scheduled to be complete at Time Now. The earned value should include all work actually finished as well as the completed portion of all work in progress. Therefore it is important that the administrator is trained thoroughly in a classroom environment, say in a full-day workshop. The members of the project team will also benefit from a half-day appreciation course. The detailed requirements of EVM should not deter the reader from its merits for implementation. It is recommended that EVM should be applied with appropriate training in larger projects.

INFORMATION AND COMMUNICATION TECHNOLOGY

Information Technology (IT) is rapidly changing and becoming more powerful. It will be a continuing source of competitive advantage for manufacturers if used correctly. In 2007 the personal computer (PC) on the desk of an average operations manager has the capability of 1,024 megabytes of main memory and 80 gigabytes of direct access storage. Ignoring the technical jargon, let's look at the facts in another way: most of us now have on our desktop more computing power than the average £100 million a year manufacturing plant had just 12 years ago. This IT revolution is available to everyone and how a company puts it to work will determine to a great extent its competitiveness in the global market.

The rapid growth of information technology has also created a number of problems and challenges. Many senior managers of companies lack any detailed understanding of the complexity of technology. They either follow the fashion (e.g. 'no one was fired for choosing IBM') or they are discouraged by the cost of technology, or by a lack of evidence of savings in a new field. When executives read about all the clever things seemingly low-cost computer technology can do they feel frustrated when systems experts say things like 'It will take three years to develop the software.' Most senior managers also feel lost in a blizzard of buzzwords. Yet another issue is the implementation of systems to the benefit of its users. When a company looks for an IT solution to a problem without re-engineering the process, refining the existing database or training the end users, the application is doomed to failure. Real disasters can be very expensive. For example the $60 million Master Trust accounting system for the Bank of America had to be scrapped because it could not maintain accurate accounts.

With the increasing use of computers and computerised systems, particularly over the last two decades, we have become increasingly accustomed to both the problems and opportunities of sharing data on project activities and members of the supply chain. The impact of information and communication technology in managing a project supply chain is demonstrated in two areas of information systems:

- Project and portfolio management
- Enterprise resource planning.

Project and Portfolio Management

The computer systems in project management are traditionally focused on time and cost control, critical path scheduling and Gantt charts. There are many such project management systems in extensive use and the most popular of these processes are Microsoft Project and Primavera by Oracle. In the 1990s, focus was generally on the management of a single project, whereas now within an organisation there are likely to be several ventures running concurrently. One project will live among many others in the enterprise, or may be part of a programme of undertakings and might utilise resources that are shared among these other projects.

In order to facilitate governance, it has become essential to be able to manage, monitor and assess the status of all schemes in the enterprise through a set of Enterprise Project Management (EPM) processes, methods and application packages. The corporate network environment is no longer tied to a single vendor, let alone a single platform. A typical enterprise project management system operates from a project management office and communicates with team members working on different tasks in the organisation; it is yet to expand its collaborative capability to external suppliers and supply chain partners in a major assignment.

Microsoft Project Server 2010 claims to bring together the business collaboration services of Microsoft Project and also unifies Project and Portfolio Management (PPM) to help major project organisations align resources and investments with the priorities of their endeavour. In MS Project 2010, portfolio management techniques are included with end-to-end project and portfolio management capabilities. Depending on the life cycle of the venture, MS Project Server 2010 provides functionalities including:

- Demand Management
- Business Case Definition
- Capacity Planning
- Portfolio Prioritisation
- Schedule Management
- Resource Management
- Project Team Collaboration
- Project Reporting.

The core processes of the Microsoft PPM system are shown in Figure 5.1. The span of each module in MS PPM varies in the life cycle phases according to its functionality and application. The demand management module is applicable during the initiation stage of the project, while project team collaboration is used during the total duration of the project. Furthermore the usage of each module could also vary according to the function and responsibility of project team members as illustrated in Figure 5.2.

There are many reports involved in each module. As an example, Figure 5.3 shows the precedence relationship of activities and resource utilisation to both proposed and allocated work.

Microsoft appears to offer a comprehensive application of information modules to manage project supply chains and also visualise performance through powerful dashboards. Oracle is offering a competitive product in its Primavera Enterprise Project Portfolio Solutions (PEPPS). This software package includes:

- Enterprise Project Portfolio Management
- Professional Project Management
- Risk Analysis
- Contract Management
- Earned Value Management.

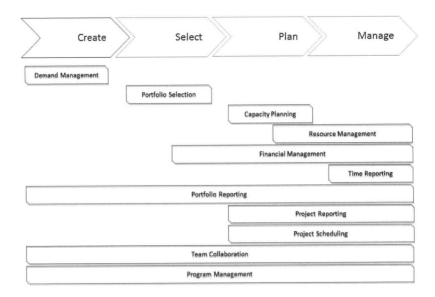

Figure 5.1   MS Project PPM modules across the project life cycle (reproduced with the kind permission of Microsoft)

How Microsoft PPM Helps The Organization

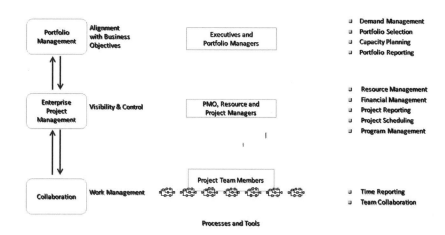

Figure 5.2   The usage of MS PPM modules by project team members (reproduced with the kind permission of Microsoft)

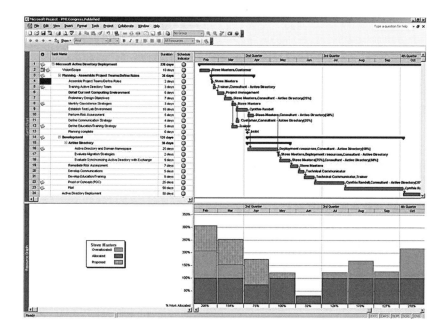

Figure 5.3   A sample page of MS Project (reproduced with the kind permission of Microsoft)

Similarly to MS Project, Oracle Primavera allows project team members to replace multiple spreadsheets with a single end-to-end database for all project information. Primavera P6 Enterprise Project Portfolio Management is an integrated PPM application that helps organisations select the right strategic mix of project, balance resource capacity, manage risk and provide management with a real-time view of the organisation's project performance. Thus for resource and risk management in particular, Primavera solutions tend to be more popular with users.

Enterprise Resource Planning

In spite of the comprehensive and extended functionalities of Microsoft Project and Oracle Primavera there appear to be significant difficulties in sharing information on procurement between members of the supply chain in a major project. Let's think about why this should be. Firstly, information exists in many locations and is typically in a raw form which is not useful for an enterprise system. Secondly, local knowledge is not formalised, although there will be a large amount of design and procurement information represented online. This leads to long meetings between parties and gives rise to instances of miscommunication. O'Brien (2001) proposes further research on enabling technologies to address these issues and problems of data sharing in three areas: extracting supply chain data, formalising local knowledge and sharing product/process visualisation.

Organisations managing major projects have been encouraged by the experience of traditional supply chain managers in Collaborative Planning Forecasting and Replenishment (CPFR) between manufacturers, suppliers and retailers. Thus they are now seeking solutions from Enterprise Resource Planning (ERP) systems on data sharing among supply chain members. ERP was designed at a time when process management was an internal affair. Companies could link their ERP systems through expensive Electronic Data Interchange (EDI) connections. Web-enabled technologies have now progressed to create e-supply chains. The market for managing the core ERP information (orders, inventory etc.) of the 'extended supply chain' is only now beginning to emerge in major projects, as the following case example illustrates.

Case example: ERP in British Columbia Transmission Corporation major projects

The British Columbia Transmission Corporation (BCTC) is a provincial Crown corporation of Canada, incorporated on 2 May 2003. BCTC's corporate offices are located in Vancouver. The corporation operates six System Control Centres all over BC, which are responsible for maintaining the reliability of the 'backbone' of BC's transmission grid, which includes 18,000 kilometres of high-voltage wires.

Upon receiving approval from the British Columbia Utilities Commission (BCUC), BCTC directed new transmission infrastructure investment projects. The Commission continues to regulate the terms and rates for transmission services.

BCTC selected IBM Business Consulting Services to lead a consortium to implement Oracle Applications version 11.5.9. IBM executed the project in two waves:

- Wave 1 consisted of the Oracle General Ledger, Fixed Assets, Accounts Receivable, Accounts Payable, Purchasing and e-Procurement modules, as well as Oracle Projects, Oracle Discoverer, Oracle Enterprise Asset Management (limited functionality) and integration with BC Hydro, banks and other BCTC systems using Oracle Interconnect.
- Wave 2 consisted of the Oracle e-Expenses and Oracle Internal Controls Manager modules, as well as some extensions to Wave 1 functionality.

In the project, IBM led a team that included up to 33 clients and 27 consultants (including Oracle Consulting and Delinea as subcontractors) and also worked with an outside infrastructure application service provider.

The fully integrated solution that IBM implemented is delivering benefits in BCTC's major project management. This includes better access to information: e.g. Oracle Discoverer enables users to build reports on their own without technical support. Furthermore due to the fact that BCTC's asset data is now segregated from BC Hydro's, BCTC can perform data analysis more easily, thus improving the quality of its decision making.

Source: IBM Business Management Consultancy (2004)

It is useful to note that SAP AG, the largest supplier of ERP systems in the world, is marketing ERP systems specifically designed for major capital projects. SAP for Engineering, Construction & Operations (SAP for EC&O), one of SAP's 23 industry solution portfolios, supports the business processes of project-oriented companies involved in the engineering, planning, execution, operation and maintenance of capital-intensive projects. Engineering firms and construction businesses are typically involved in costly, high-risk projects. They are organised in a decentralised structure which demands a solution allowing high integration and close collaboration both within the enterprise and across global supply chains and partner networks.

Collaborative Planning Forecasting and Replenishment (CPFR, or just 'collaborative forecasting') is the process of setting up a continual line of communication between yourself and those customers with the ability to predict the future needs of the products they buy from you. Advances in electronic commerce have facilitated better communications between computer systems that have resulted in the development of electronic CPFR systems. Large retailers like Wal-Mart and Tesco are benefiting from sophisticated CPFR systems by electronic links with the major suppliers' ERP and Global Supply Chain systems.

In the case of project supply chains it may not be necessary to introduce sophisticated e-supply chain or CPFR systems with all members of the supply chain. However the principles of CPFR and Sales & Operations Planning (S&OP) can be gainfully incorporated in the supply chain of major projects. The Supply Chain Manager in a major project should take the role of coordinating S&OP style regular and formal meetings between the supply chain members (including major suppliers) of the project. The objectives of these S&OP style meetings are different from a typical project review meeting insomuch as here the emphasis is on collaborative forecasting and rough cut capacity planning.

The supply chain related problems in major projects such Airbus 380 or London Olympic 2012 could be contained and resolved by a formal collaborative forecasting process between key suppliers and stakeholders of the project. The benefits are more significant when the supply chain members are electronically linked to share the common data. Even in smaller projects, collaborative forecasting can deliver huge benefits, as the following case example illustrates.

Case example: collaborative forecasting in Dower projects

Dower Industries uses a No. 456 gasket in the process of rebuilding a No. A 4000 power unit. On average, Dower rebuilds two power units each month and the building of each one is considered to be a project because the No. A4000 power unit is critical to Dower's operations. Its supplier, Ajax Distribution, normally keeps four No. 456 gaskets in stock.

However in a specific month – say, September – Dower's engineers decide they need to rebuild eight power units in November. Although the No. 456 gasket is a critical component in the rebuilding process, it is only a small element of the total procedure. Ajax Distribution always has an ample supply of gaskets in stock, so it doesn't occur to Dower's buyer to notify Ajax of the increased need for the product occurring in eight weeks' time.

On 1 November, Dower starts rebuilding the power units. After completing four units, they're stopped dead in the water because there are no more gaskets. Dower's management strongly voices its displeasure at the buyer, who in turn unloads on his contact at Ajax. Ajax offers excuses, citing the unusual and sudden level of demand and offers to increase its normal inventory of No. 456 gaskets from four pieces to eight. The result: Ajax has disappointed the customer and brought in additional stock that is probably excess inventory.

This situation could have been avoided if Ajax and Dower implemented a programme to exchange need and availability information. Using a CPFR system, Dower would have notified Ajax of the increased need for the gaskets as soon as it made the decision to accelerate maintenance operations. Ajax would have ordered more gaskets for a late October or early November delivery. Following this experience Dower set up an EDI link with Ajax and a simple process of CPFR was established in Dower projects.

Source: www.effectiveinventory.com (2006)

The applications that support project-based processes within an organisation are commonly referred to as Professional Services Automation (PSA) solutions. PSA solutions appear to be very much in vogue in the field of project performance improvement at the moment. PSA solutions comprise a range of specific modules that combine to provide an answer to manage the entire project life cycle. The integrated nature of the PSA modules supports and enhances the flow of real-time information throughout a business collecting detailed transactional data accurately and turning it into business knowledge that can be shared to business benefit. PSA solutions are offered to project organisations as functional packages such as Customer Relationship Management (CRM), Human Resources Management (HRM), (Project Delivery Management (PDM), Project Execution Management (PEM), (Project Cost Management (PCM) etc.

In a recent study Cap Gemini (2005) surveyed a number of projects where PSA solutions had been used. On each result the following four areas were addressed:

- Internal Perspective (the organisation features of the PSA vendor)
- External Perspective (customer side of the solution)
- Technical Perspective (technical aspects of the system)
- Functional Perspective (how well the solution fulfilled the requirements of process areas).

Their report showed that 42 per cent of PSA vendors had disappeared in the last five years, but most of the solutions had been adopted by new vendors. Our critical observation on PSA solutions is that they are useful data management systems but that their effectiveness in achieving operational excellence in projects depends on how their outputs are used for project performance improvement. The demise of 42 per cent of vendors in five years indicates only a moderate success rate of PSA solutions.

SUMMARY

This chapter has covered the systems and procedures that help to integrate the activities of the building blocks in the project supply chain. The appropriateness of the guidelines in bodies of knowledge – e.g. PMBOK (2008), PRINCE2 (2009) – and the specific roles of NEC3 (2005) have been examined. The specific role of NEC 3 (2005) has been discussed in Chapter 4.

With financial management we introduce key concepts and ratios. Unless the project manager understands these ratios he or she will always be at the mercy of the accountants. The figures are explained simply and illustrated with easily understood examples. If you have some accounting knowledge, don't skip this section – take five minutes to work through the examples and consider how they apply to your organisation.

For information technology we have taken a more general approach. This section is equally applicable to all functions of the organisation. The key issue in any new IT system is knowing what you want, going with a system with local support and initially making do with off-the-shelf software. We have not discussed the uninterrupted power supply, disaster recovery, the need to back up files etc. All these issues are 'nuts and bolts' and should be second nature to your IT manager. This section was not written for the professional IT executive. Rather, it was designed to give the average manager an understanding of the strategy of IT implementation applications in managing project supply chains.

CHAPTER 6

SUPPLY CHAIN INTEGRATION: QUALITY AND PERFORMANCE MANAGEMENT

INTRODUCTION

In this chapter the role of quality and performance management systems in integrating the building blocks and processes in project supply chains is discussed. The review of literature (Basu, 2010) indicates that quality is mostly a 'lip service' or ticking of boxes in project management. There should be a clearer definition of project quality to establish some key dimensions, and then some appropriate processes in managing project supply chains.

WHAT IS QUALITY IN SUPPLY CHAIN MANAGEMENT?

Quality in supply chain management has two stages, a basic level and a higher rank. At the basic level common definitions such as 'fitness for purpose', 'getting it right first time' and 'right thing, right place, right time' apply. (These classifications have all been so overused that they have almost become clichés.) In other words to meet our perception of quality there are certain basic requirements that have to be met, and there are certain higher-order conditions that must be realised.

At a higher level, there are many different definitions and dimensions of quality to be found in books and academic literature. We will present three of these descriptions selected from published literature and propose a three-dimensional explanation of quality. One of the most respected definitions of quality is given by the eight quality dimensions (see Table 6.1) developed by David Garvin of the Harvard Business School (1984).

Table 6.1   Garvin's product quality dimensions

Performance	The efficiency (e.g. return on investment) with which the product achieves its intended purpose.
Features	Attributes that supplement the product's basic performance, e.g. tinted glass windows in a car.
Reliability	The capability of the product to perform consistently over its life cycle.
Conformance	Meeting the specifications of the product, usually defined by numeric values.
Durability	The degree to which a product withstands stress without failure.
Serviceability	Used to denote the ease of repair.
Aesthetics	Sensory characteristics such as look, sound, taste and smell.
Perceived quality	Is based on customer opinion.

The above dimensions of quality are not mutually exclusive, although they relate primarily to the quality of the product. Neither are they exhaustive. Service quality is perhaps even more difficult to define than product quality. A set of service quality dimensions (see Table 6.2) that is widely cited has been compiled by Parasuraman et al. (1984).

Table 6.2   Parasuraman et al. service quality dimensions

Tangibles	The physical appearance of the service facility and people.
Service reliability	The ability of the service provider to perform dependably.
Responsiveness	The willingness of the service provider to be prompt in delivering the service.
Assurance	The ability of the service provider to inspire trust and confidence.
Empathy	The ability of the service provider to demonstrate care and individual attention to the customer.
Availability	The ability to provide service at the right time and place.
Timeliness	The delivery of service within the agreed lead time.
Professionalism	Encompasses the impartial and ethical characteristics of the service provider.
Completeness	Addresses the delivery of the order in full.
Pleasantness	Simply means good manners and politeness.

Another definition of quality is taken from Wild (2002, p. 644):

> *The quality of a product or service is the degree to which it satisfies customer*
> *requirements. It is influenced by:*
> *Design quality: the degree to which the* specification *of the product or service*
> *satisfies customers' requirements.*
> *Process quality: the degree to which the product or service, which is made*
> *available to the customer,* conforms *to specification.*

The list of quality dimensions by both Garvin and Parasuraman et al. are widely cited and respected. However, one problem with definitions is that if time permitted, the reader would find several other useful definitions and dimensions. Wild's definition of design/process quality does provide a broad framework to develop a company specific quality strategy.

Nonetheless, one important dimension of quality is not clearly visible in the above models: the quality of the organisation. This is a fundamental cornerstone of the value of a holistic process and an essential requirement of an approved quality assessment scheme such as the European Foundation of Quality Management (EFQM). Therefore, a three-dimensional model of quality has been developed (Basu, 2004), as shown in diagrammatic form in Figure 6.1.

When an organisation develops and defines its quality strategy, it is important to share a common definition of quality, and each department within a company can work towards a common objective. The product quality should contain defined attributes of both numeric specifications and perceived dimensions. The process quality, whether it relates to manufacturing or service operations, should also contain some defined criteria of acceptable service level so that the conformity

Figure 6.1   Three dimensions of quality

of the output can be validated against these criteria. Perhaps the most important determinant of how we perceive sustainable quality is the functional and holistic role that we as individuals have within the organisation. Organisation quality can only germinate when the approach is holistic and a single set of numbers based on transparent measurement is emphasised with senior management commitment. We have compiled a set of key organisation quality dimensions (see Table 6.3).

Table 6.3   Basu's organisation quality dimensions

Top Management Commitment	Organisational quality cannot exist without the total commitment of the top executive team.
Sales and Operations Planning	A monthly senior management review process to align strategic objectives with operation tasks.
Single Set of Numbers	Provides the common business data for all functions in the company.
Using Appropriate Tools and Techniques	Relates to the fact that without the effective application of appropriate tools and techniques, the speed of improvement will not be assured.
Performance Management	Includes the selection, measurement, monitoring and application of Key Performance Indicators.
Knowledge Management	Comprises the education, training and development of employees, sharing of best practice and communication media.
Teamwork Culture	Requires that team work should be practised in cross-functional groups to encourage a borderless organisation.
Self-assessment	Enables a regular health check of all aspects of the organisation against a checklist or accepted assessment process such as EFQM.
Continuous Learning	An ongoing learning process that seeks to incorporate the lessons learnt (from the results of already achieved) into a continuous improvement programme.

Hierarchy of Quality

With the subject of quality, like many management subjects such as marketing and strategic management, a number of technical terms have evolved. In this section we discuss the various ways in which quality can be managed. We also examine the strengths and weaknesses of each technique. For these reasons we have developed a hierarchy of methods of quality management. Our hierarchy approximates the evolution of quality management from simple testing to a full total Quality Management System (QMS).

Quality Inspection

Traditionally the concept of quality was conformance to certain dimensions and specifications, the cliché being 'fitness for purpose'. Quality control was achieved by inspection and supervision. Inspection is the most basic approach to quality, the aim being for an inspector to detect – and if sufficiently serious to reject – before despatch in order to ascertain if a product deviates from a set standard. Inspection will at least provide the customer with an acceptable product. Quality inspection is an expensive method of achieving a basic level of quality. It requires the employment of people to check on the operators. Inspection and supervision do not add value to a product, but they do add to the cost.

The stage of production where the inspection takes place is important. If the only scrutiny is at the end of the production line then, if deviations from the standard are discovered at this late stage, the cost of reworking could well double the cost of the item. If a divergence from standard is not spotted, the final inspector is the customer, by which time it is too late. If the product is found to be below criterion by the customer, the manufacturer has the problem of putting it right. This correction process could include the cost of scrapping the unit and giving the client a new one, or in extreme cases a total product recall with all the costs and loss of consumer confidence that this entails.

Quality inspection at a more advanced level includes checking and testing at various stages of production so that errors can be identified early and remedial action taken before the next stage of the process takes place. At a still higher level of assessment, materials are examined on receipt and then probably tested again before being drawn from the store. Of course all these tests and checks take time and cost money. The cost is easy to quantify when the analyses are carried out by people whose prime job is to gauge and verify the work of others. The costs of relying on inspection by people other than the operator are therefore two-fold:

1. A level of error becomes accepted as standard and is included in the price.
2. Inspectors do not add value to the product. Inspectors are in themselves an added cost.

The next stage beyond quality inspection can be designated quality control.

Quality Control

With quality control, the aim is not only to monitor the quality at various stages of the process but also to identify and eliminate the causes of unsatisfactory quality so that they do not happen again. Whereas inspection is an 'after the fact' approach, quality control is aimed at preventing mistakes. With quality control, you would expect to find in place drawings, raw material testing, intermediate process assessment, some self-inspection by workers, a process of keeping of records of failure, and some feedback to supervisors and operators regarding errors and percentage of errors. The end aims are to reduce waste by eliminating mistakes and to make sure that production reaches a specified level of quality before shipment to the customer.

Quality Assurance

Quality assurance includes all the steps taken under quality control and quality inspection. It includes, where appropriate, the setting of standards with documentation for dimensions, tolerances, machine settings, raw material grades, operating temperatures and any other safety quality or standard that might be desirable. Quality assurance would also include the documentation of the method of checking against the specified standards. Quality assurance generally includes a continuous training programme. With quality assurance one would expect to move from the detection of errors to the correction of process so as to prevent errors. One would also expect a comprehensive quality manual, the recording of failures to achieve quality standards and costs, the use of statistical process control (SPC) and the audit of quality systems.

Total Quality Management

The fourth and highest level in our hierarchy of quality is Total Quality Management (TQM). The lower levels of quality inspection, quality control and quality assurance are aimed at achieving an agreed consistent level of quality, first by testing and inspection, then by rigid conformance to standards and procedures, and finally by efforts to eliminate the causes of errors so that the defined and accepted level of quality will be achieved. However, this is a cold and sterile approach to quality. It implies that once a sufficient level of quality has been achieved, then apart from maintaining that stage, which in itself might be hard work, little more needs to be done. This is often the western approach to quality and has its roots in Taylorism (see Taylor, 1997).

Total quality management is on a different plane. Total quality management does, of course, include all the previous levels of setting standards and the means of measuring conformance to standards. In doing this, SPC will be used, systems will be documented and accurate and timely feedback of results will be given. With TQM, ISO accreditation might be sought, but an organisation that truly has embraced TQM will not need the ISO stamp of approval.

Any organisation aspiring to TQM will have a vision of quality which goes far beyond mere conformity with a standard. TQM requires a culture whereby every member of the organisation believes that not one day should go by without the organisation in some way improving the quality of its goods and services. The vision of TQM must begin with the chief executive. If this chief executive has a passion for quality and continuous improvement, and if this enthusiasm can be transmitted down through the organisation, then, paradoxically, the ongoing driving force will be from the bottom up. TQM, however, goes beyond the staff of the organisation – it goes outside the establishment and involves suppliers, customers and the general public.

Once a relationship has been built with a supplier, then they are no longer treated with suspicion or, in some cases, almost as an adversary. Instead of trying to get the best deal possible out of the supplier, instead they become a member of the team. The supplier gains involvement in the day-to-day problems and concerns of the organisation and is expected to assist, help and advise. The supplier also becomes part of the planning team. Price and discounts will no longer be the crucial issues. Instead the delivery of the correct materials at the right time will be the real concerns, and suppliers will be judged accordingly. Once a supplier proves reliable, the checking and testing of inwards goods will become less critical. Ideally, the level of trust will be such that the raw materials can be delivered direct to the operator's workplace rather than to a central store.

The cost of TQM can be measured in monetary terms. The emphasis will be on prevention rather than detection, thus the cost of supervision and inspection will go down. Prevention cost will rise due to training and action-orientated efforts. But the real benefits will be gained by a significant reduction in failures – both internal (e.g. scrap, rework, downtime) and external (handling of complaints, servicing costs, loss of goodwill). The total operating cost will reduce over time (say, three to five years), as shown in Figure 6.2.

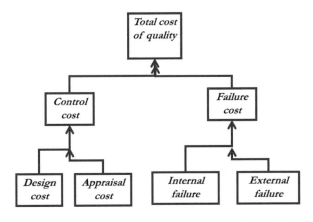

Figure 6.2   Total cost of quality

The adoption of a standard such as ISO 9000, rather than streamlining an organisation, might actually serve to increase the need for audits and supervision. Therefore to this extent ISO 9000 can be seen to be contrary to the philosophy of TQM. With TQM, staff members are encouraged to do their own checking and to be responsible for getting it right first time. Thus the need for supervision becomes almost superfluous. With ISO 9000, the standard method is likely to be set by management edict and, once put in place, the bureaucracy of agreeing and recording improvements may stultify creative advances and progress.

TQM TO FIT SIGMA™

'Today, depending on whom you listen to, Six Sigma is either a revolution slashing trillions of dollars from corporate inefficiency, or it's the most maddening management fad yet, devised to keep front-line workers too busy collecting data to do their jobs' (*USA Today*, 21 July 1998).

It has been several years since the above statement was made. During this time the 'Six Sigma revolution' has created a huge impact in the field of Operational Excellence, yet conflicting views are still prevalent.

Let us evaluate the arguments for both sides. On a positive note, the success of Six Sigma in General Electric (GE) under the leadership of Jack Welch is undisputed. In the GE company report of 2000 their CEO was unstinting in his praise: 'Six Sigma has galvanised our company with an intensity the likes of which I have never seen in my 40 years of GE' (Basu and Wright, 2004, p. 54). Even financial analysts and investment bankers compliment the success of Six Sigma in GE. An analyst at Morgan Stanley, Dean Witter, recently estimated that GE's gross annual benefit from Six Sigma could reach five per cent of sales and that share value might increase by between 10 and 15 per cent (Best Practices LLC, 2000, p. 46).

However the situation is more complex than such predictions would suggest. In spite of the demonstrated benefits of many improvement techniques – such as total quality management, Business Process Re-Engineering and Six Sigma – most attempts by companies to use them have ended in failure (Easton and Jarrell, 1998). Sterman et al. (1999) conclude that companies have found it extremely difficult to sustain even initially successful process improvement initiatives. Yet more puzzling is the fact that successful improvement programmes have sometimes led to declining business performance, causing lay-offs and low employee morale. Motorola, the originator of Six Sigma, announced in 1998 that its second-quarter profit was almost non-existent and that consequently it was cutting 15,000 of its 150,000 jobs.

To counter heavyweight enthusiasts like Jack Welch (GE) and Larry Bossidy (Allied Signal) there are sharp critics of Six Sigma. Although Six Sigma may sound new, critics say that it is really Statistical Process Control in new clothing. Others dismiss it as another transitory management fad that will soon pass. It is evident that like any good product Six Sigma should also have a finite life cycle. In addition, Business Managers can be forgiven if they are often confused by the grey areas of distinction between quality initiatives such as TQM, Six Sigma and Lean Sigma.

Against this background, let us examine the evolution of total quality improvement processes (or in a broader sense Operational Excellence) from Ad-hoc Improvement to TQM to Six Sigma to Lean Sigma. Building on the success factors of these processes, the key question is: how do we sustain the results? The authors have named this sustainable process FIT SIGMA (see Basu and Wright, 2004; Basu, 2011).

So, what is FIT SIGMA? Firstly, take the key ingredient of quality, then add accuracy in the order of no more than 3.4 defects in 1 million. Now implement this across your business with an intensive education and training programme. The result is Six Sigma. Now let's look at Lean Enterprise, an updated version of classical Industrial Engineering. It focuses on delivered value from a customer's perspective and strives to eliminate all non-value-added activities ('waste') for each product or service along a value chain. The integration of the complementary approaches of Six Sigma and Lean Enterprise is known as 'Lean Sigma'. FIT SIGMA is the next wave. If Lean Sigma provides agility and efficiency, then FIT SIGMA allows a sustainable fitness. In addition the control of variation from the mean (small Sigma 'σ') in the Six Sigma process is transformed to a companywide integration (capital Sigma 'Σ') in the FIT SIGMA process. Furthermore, the philosophy of FIT SIGMA should ensure that it is indeed 'fit' for the organisation.

WHAT IS QUALITY IN PROJECT MANAGEMENT?

The extant project management literature (Turner, 1999; Atkinson, 1999; Meredith and Mantel, 2003) identifies three objectives for assessing the success of a project – known as the 'iron triangle' of time, cost and quality. The first two aims are relatively simple to define and measure (Morris, 1997). Project quality as the third dimension of the 'iron triangle' is more difficult to characterise and assess, although it has received some attention in the academic literature (Turner, 2007; Heisler, 1990). Turner is among the few authors who have attempted to define project quality comprising two dimensions: product quality and process quality. The guidelines for project quality in the *Body of Knowledge* (APM, 2006; PMI, 2008; PRINCE2, 2009) also reflect only paper-based procedures of design and process requirements. These definitions and guidelines fail due to their lack of clarity and organisation learning practices (Kotnour, 2000)

The opacity surrounding quality is often the source of project disputes and there are in fact numerous reports in the business world – e.g. National Audit Office (2000); Transport Select Committee (2008); British and Irish Legal Information Institute (www.bailii.org, accessed 26 November 2008) – documenting the link between inadequate attention to quality management and unsuccessful major projects. When we search the domain of operations management we may observe some proven paths to follow. As discussed earlier in this chapter, the area of operations management enjoys some success stories (along with failures) of the application of quality-based operational excellence concepts such as total quality management, Six Sigma, lean and supply chain management (Oakland, 2003).

The application of operational excellence concepts are now extended to non-manufacturing processes: 'Firms such as Motorola, [and] General Electric … successfully implemented Six Sigma. Motorola saved $15 billion in an 11 year period. General Electric saved $2 billion in 1999 alone … Although Six Sigma initiatives have focused primarily on improving the performance of manufacturing processes, the concepts are widely applied in non-manufacturing, administrative and service functions' (Weinstein et al. 2008, p. 233). Even though operational excellence models (such as Six Sigma) are often driven by the objective of cost effectiveness, the enablers of these concepts are rooted to the fundamentals of quality management (Oakland, 2003).

In the domain of operations management, the dimensions and definitions of quality have been identified by some authors (Garvin, 1984; Parasuraman et al. 1984). The early leaders of total quality management (Deming, 1986; Juran, 1989; Feigenbaum, 1983) emphasised the importance of people-related issues as a dimension of quality. On the other hand, the dimensions and definitions of quality appear to be wanting in publications related to project management. Indeed, project management standards (e.g. PMBOK, 2008; PRINCE2, 2009) focus primarily on processes in the project life cycle, with only some references to quality management systems. Turner (2007) appears to agree with Wild's dimensions of product quality and process quality. Kotnour (2000) points out the lack of clarity in the definition of project quality and the role of organisational learning in project management. There are publications regarding the success criteria and success factors of projects (Pinto and Slevin, 1988; Grude et al. 1996) but their implications in the dimensions of project quality are not clear. The application of excellence models in projects does appear to be limited (Westerveld, 2003). Unlike operations management, the tools and concepts of operations excellence (Basu, 2004), such as Lean and Six Sigma, are rarely being applied in project management (Pinch, 2005)

An empirical study by Basu (2009) validates project quality with three dimensions comprising design, process and organisation. This underpins project excellence with project quality, operational excellence concepts and continuous assessment. The broad acceptability of dimensions of quality by project managers was tested through the administration of an online questionnaire and trial of a deductive causal Partial Least Squares (PLS) model. The survey findings were augmented and corroborated by two case studies of contemporary infrastructure projects (viz. Heathrow Terminal 5 and Channel Tunnel High Speed 1). Figure 6.3 shows the model of project quality and project excellence.

In line with the model (Figure 6.3) and further analysis of the two case studies, a checklist for the Assessment of Project Excellence, named APEX, has been developed under the six major constructs/components/categories of project quality and excellence as follows:

1. Quality Management Systems and Procedures
2. Quality Audits and Compliance
3. Performance Management
4. Organisation Effectiveness
5. Operational Excellence Concepts and Applications
6. Self-Assessment and Knowledge Management.

APEX Model
Assessing Project Excellence

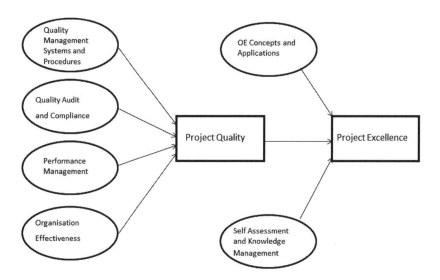

Figure 6.3   Project quality and excellence model

Each component or construct comprises five questions or items in the checklist. This inventory has been carefully constructed on the basis of findings from the literature review, field research and case studies. There are 30 questions in total (five questions in each category) which are ranked on a scale of one to five, where 1 equals not important and 5 equals most important. With the aid of these questions in the APEX model (www.rbcon.co.uk) at any stage of the project life cycle the quality management processes can be reviewed. This is carried out as a self-assessment exercise by quality managers to identify gaps for continuous improvement.

It is also important that each major project should have a dedicated quality function with a budget and a written quality management system. Quality strategy and procedures contribute to the QMS framework to set and deliver quality requirements by systematically integrating quality planning, quality assurance, quality control and quality improvement processes in a project. Figure 6.4 shows the structure of QMS adopted in a recent major project in the UK.

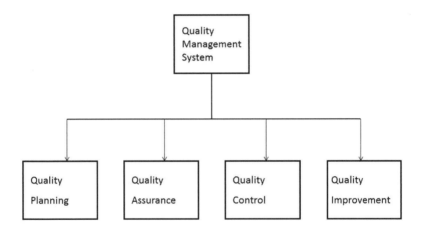

Figure 6.4   Structure of a quality management system (reproduced with the kind permission of BAA)

PERFORMANCE MANAGEMENT

The performance management system of a major project is underpinned by well-designed Key Performance Indicators (KPIs) and Measures. The KPIs are selected as high-level quality indicators to steer the major project objectives and requirements. The KPIs, supported by linked key measures, provide overall snapshots to direct the project through enablers, monitoring progress or assuring results. The Performance Data are the metrics which are measured for each part of the project by team members, including suppliers, to monitor performance as a target or planned versus actual. Finally, the key measures are the chosen 10 measures to be reported and published regularly.

It is important to recognise that all metrics must be tried and tested with worked-out examples. In addition they should be validated by collecting trial data under different conditions before they are communicated to the project team. It is helpful to provide a guidance note for each metric which can then be explained to team members in workshops to gain their understanding and acceptance. A similar process was followed for Heathrow Terminal 5 (T5) performance metrics and a Quality KPI workbook was prepared (Basu et al. 2009). The workbook contained a description and definition of each indicator and measure supported by guidance notes and individual or team roles. In order to clearly assign responsibility and accountability for each KPI, a simple RACI (responsible, accountable, consult and inform) format was used. Each team member or leader, either as an individual or as a team, was aware of their role as a Sponsor (responsible), Owner (accountable), Contributor (consult) or Participant (inform). The roll-out and implementation of the Balanced Scorecard based performance management for the T5 project was enabled and enhanced by two major initiatives of the project. As part of the 'T5 Agreement' contractors were liable for the relevant key performance measures.

It is these key performance measures that provide a snapshot of the operation of each project team. They were also highlighted by red, amber, green (RAG) colour codes according to their status with regard to targets. However, improvement projects were acted upon more by individual performance measures at the specific project level. The most significant contributors to improvement projects were Non-Conformance Reports (NCRs). There were nine performance measures related to NCRs as part of one KPI, viz. Compliance Assured. These measures enabled the quantification of a part of 'Cost of Poor Quality' (COPQ) given by the Estimated Cost of NCRs. Root Cause Analyses by type of non-conformance and supplier led to continuous improvement in design, processes and savings. Overall around 6,000 non-conformance reports were raised on T5, but the accumulative cost of non-conformance was only 0.6 per cent of the budget. Analysis of the data showed that 70 per cent of the total cost of non-conformance resulted from just 150 reports. A 'no blame' culture led to the speedy and effective resolution of all issues.

As discussed above, key performance indicators and key measures of the T5 project were customised to meet the requirements of the T5 Agreement and the complexity of the project spanning rail, road and air infrastructures. However, the key balancing principles of the four aspects (Financial, Customer, Internal Processes and Learning and Growth) of the Kaplan and Norton Balanced Scorecard (Kaplan and Norton, 1996) have been incorporated in the T5 KPIs as shown in Figure 6.5.

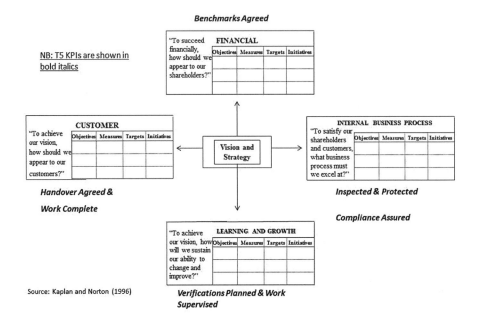

Figure 6.5   T5 Balanced Scorecard (reproduced with the kind permission of BAA)

In the Kaplan and Norton Balanced Scorecard, the enabling or leading indicators are 'Financial' and 'Learning and Growth'. Looking at the T5 Balanced Scorecard, the enabling indicators are 'Benchmarks Agreed' (which also include some financial yardsticks) and 'Verifications Planned and Work Supervised' (containing supervisor's training). As regards the lagging or results indicators, 'Handover Agreed and Work Complete' in T5 relates to the 'Customer' aspect of Kaplan and Norton, while the T5 KPIs, 'Inspected and Protected' and 'Compliance Assured', pertain to Kaplan and Norton's 'Internal Process' section.

Arguably there are some gaps in the T5 Key Performance Indicators and the Key Measures related to the 'financial' and 'growth' (innovation) aspects, but the manufacturing and assembly stage KPIs would not be expected to address this.

The metrics of the T5 Balanced Scorecard have been designed to reflect the specific requirements of the project as enablers, as well as showing results leading to continuous improvement. The experience of the project team indicates that NCR-related data has been most effective in the identification of the cost of poor quality; to improve design and processes by analysing root causes by task or supplier; and also to attract the attention of the project board.

It is evident from the experience of the T5 performance management system that the fundamental principles of the Balanced Scorecard have been gainfully adopted and customised to the performance management systems of T5. They have been tailored in order to meet the specific requirements of this complex major project. It can be seen that the best practices of project performance management arising from this case study include:

- Encouraging supplier partnership and the proactive involvement of contractors in monitoring and improving project quality and conformance to standards.
- Providing indicators and measures within three main themes as enablers, monitoring progress and showing results along the project life cycle, right up to the handover and completion of work.
- The metrics and processes are validated and then embedded by extensive discussions with stakeholders, followed by documentation, communication campaign and training workshops.
- The ongoing testimony of non-conformance reports (NCRs), supported by the estimation of the cost of non-conformance and improvement projects based on root cause analysis, is a strong point of the process and opens up opportunities for Six Sigma and innovation.
- Suppliers should be empowered to own the monitoring and improvement process using their performance data. Metrics should be customised within the framework of the Kaplan and Norton Balanced Scorecard.

SUMMARY

In this chapter we have examined the role of quality as an integrator. We have shown that quality management has three dimensions – design quality, process quality and organisation quality. Furthermore 'quality' is basically what the customer wants and it operates at two levels – the basic prerequisites of specification, time and cost, and higher-level requirements covering after delivery service and customer focus issues. We accept that quality has a price, but the cost of not performing can be unknown and is probably unknowable.

We also discussed a hierarchy of quality methods, ranging from inspection at the end of the process to no inspection by supervisors and the reliance on suppliers – and the onus on each worker in the process to get it right first time, every time. For such a bold approach to be viable – e.g. no supervisors, no inspectors – workers must be empowered. But more than that, they must *want* to be empowered, and managers must believe and trust. For most companies this is a desirable goal, but probably not something to be attempted overnight. A good-quality management system should be underpinned by a properly designed Balanced Scorecard based performance management system, as the experience of the T5 project demonstrated.

CHAPTER 7

SUPPLY CHAIN INTEGRATION: REGULAR REVIEWS

INTRODUCTION

Each building block may be managed very efficiently within its own silo, but these integrating processes act as a glue to the Project Supply Chain to deliver the project at the right time, right cost and right quality. Without these processes, especially regular reviews, the synergy of all building blocks could not attain their full potential. In this chapter the key processes of how to optimise reviews by appropriate groups at appropriate times on the specific issues project supply chains are discussed.

WHY REVIEWS?

In the *Project Management Body of Knowledge* (PMBOK, 2008) the importance of project review meetings is recognised and well defined, as they 'provide[s] the critical links among people, ideas and information that is necessary for success'. However there are few publications available, with the exception of the OGC Gateway Review process (www.ogc.gov.uk), to provide guidelines for project review conferences. Project Managers are often divided in their opinions about the efficacy of progress meetings. Some managers prefer numerous, small, frequent meetings while others prefer the occasional big get-together with almost everyone in the project in attendance. While it is true that there are some who consider 'meetings, bloody meetings' as a time waster, many view progress conventions as forums where steps forward, issues and risks can be discussed and agreed upon.

According to the OGC website:

> The OGC Gateway Process examines programmes and projects at key decision points in their lifecycle. OGC Gateway Reviews are applicable to a wide range of programmes and projects including ... procurements using or establishing framework arrangements. The process is mandatory in central civil government ... OGC Gateway Reviews deliver a 'peer review' in which independent practitioners from outside the programme/project use

their experience and expertise to examine the progress and likelihood of the successful delivery of the programme or project. The review uses a series of interviews, documentation reviews and the team's experience to provide valuable additional perspective on the issues facing the project team, and an external challenge to the robustness of plans and processes. They are used to provide a valuable additional perspective on the issues facing the internal team, and an external challenge to the robustness of plans and processes.

Although the 'gateway' reviews provide useful additional perspectives on project issues, the need for regular and formal internal progress meetings cannot be underestimated. Sales and Operations Planning (S&OP) is an integrator of the building blocks of total supply chain management. In this method, all key managers and staff are involved in the process, but not at the same meeting. Every organisation usually has some form of regular planning meeting in which the financial and business plans are reviewed and often some marketing and operational targets are discussed by a group of managers. These monthly seminars tend to deal with short-term problems and opportunities, and usually decisions are made according to the subjective judgements of an influential senior manager. In many companies, what passes for S&OP is often little more than a monthly review of the performance of the Master Production Schedule (MPS). Many software providers also take the view that it is best done as an extension of the existing product level planning process.

In our experience both of these approaches fail to achieve the very real business benefits that an effective S&OP process can deliver. S&OP should be treated as a formal planning and execution procedure rather than just as a set of planning meetings. Whether the business processes are forecast driven, MRPII processes or order driven pull or Just-in-Time practices, the role of S&OP is equally important. Furthermore, there must be a course of action within S&OP that breaks down the aggregate plan into detailed arrangements.

Dick Ling, almost the founding father of S&OP, defines Sales and Operations Planning as a process rather than a system, saying that it is, 'the process that enables a company to integrate its planning within the total company'. The outcome of the process is the updated operation plan over 18 months or two years (the 'planning horizon') with a firm commitment for at least one month. The process involves a set of sequential reviews by process owners, starting with a demand study, then a supply and capacity appraisal followed by a reconciliation of demand and supply. Finally there should be a senior management evaluation to approve the sales and operation plan over the planning horizon. The benefits of S&OP type meetings with major suppliers and stakeholders are also applicable to project supply chains.

WHICH REVIEWS AND WHEN AND BY WHOM?

Learning from the good practices of S&OP as an integrator of supply chain management, project supply chain review meetings should also be sequential, ensuring that all key managers and staff are involved in the process but not at the same meeting. These review processes usually include:

1. Team Meeting
2. Supply Chain Review Meeting
3. Project Management Meeting
4. Milestone Review Meeting.

In addition there are Functional Meetings, Performance Review Meetings and Gateway Review Meetings to complement the mainstream review meetings as illustrated in Figure 7.1.

Team Meetings are conducted for each work package every week and are led by the team leader. The purpose of these meetings is to monitor progress and identify issues and bottlenecks to be resolved in subsequent meetings. The issues related to procurement, and its impact on the contraction schedule, are recorded for the next supply chain review meeting.

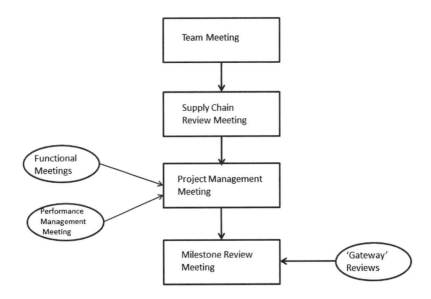

Figure 7.1   Project review meetings

Supply Chain Review Meetings are conducted every month and the key participants are the Supply Chain Manager, Buyers, the Schedule Planner and Major Contractors. The main objective of this meeting is to reconcile the issues arising from the procurement schedule (demand) and construction schedule (supply). The relevant issues developing from team meetings are also reviewed during this discussion. A typical such encounter will contain an agenda, procurement schedule, construction schedule, minutes from the previous meeting, configuration management and actions.

Project Management Meetings normally takes place prior to Milestone Review Meetings to assess the overall progress of projects and identify the key issues and any bottlenecks. The meeting is chaired by the Project Manager and the participants include Team Leaders, Functional Managers and representatives from major contractors. During this gathering it is common for process owners to give estimates or promises of fresh dates by which the issues can be resolved. Claims and accomplishments since the last meeting are also discussed.

Milestone review meetings are also known as Steering or Project Board Meetings. The participants are the Steering Team members from both Sponsors or Clients and the Project Management, including the Project Managers. In these gatherings the issues arising from the project management meetings are resolved. The milestones of the project are reviewed and monitored, and managers can compare actual costs and progress with a project budget and milestone schedules of work. A milestone denotes a particular, easily defined stage in the project schedule. Sometimes a milestone is recognised by the end of a phase in the project life cycle which is followed by a handover meeting. The purpose of the handover meeting is to formally terminate the phase or commence the next stage, or subcontract.

Functional Meetings are conducted on an 'ad hoc' or 'as required' basis. These seminars are related to Risk Management, Health Safety and Environment, Audit Review, Configuration Management and Quality Management. The risk management plan is reviewed and communicated to all project participants and, where necessary, is followed up by appropriate training. The plan is updated and changes to the scope of work, team members and suppliers are documented and passed on to project management meetings. A similar process is followed for other functions such as health, safety and environment, audit reviews and quality management.

It is essential to ensure continuous improvement in supply chain and project delivery performance by a regular review of Balanced Scorecard based Key Performance Indicators. As indicated earlier in the example of the T5 project, the review should extend to the participation by key suppliers to identify the cost of non-conformance. The outcomes and issues arising from performance reviews should be passed on to project management meetings. It is also important to establish a learning organisation culture. Unless staff at all levels are sharing in knowledge, and truly believe that the business can benefit from the exchange of ideas, the gathering of data will have achieved very little. If an organisation feels that they already know what the best practice is and are satisfied with incremental improvement then regrettably, it is fair to say that they will be left behind. History shows that knowledge progresses in leaps and bounds. The development of a learning culture does not just happen, and words are not enough.

SUMMARY

In this chapter the importance of regular reviews by progressive meetings has been explained and emphasised. Even if good systems and processes are in place the involvement and appropriate commitments of all members and key stakeholders of the project are essential for its success. This is effected by well-designed and organised review seminars so that all members are involved in the process, but not in the same meeting. In addition to traditional project review meetings S &OP style Supply Review Meetings are recommended for major projects

CHAPTER 8

LEAN AND AGILE PROJECT SUPPLY CHAIN

INTRODUCTION

In the preceding chapters the benefits of managing major projects by embedding the traditional best practices of Supply Chain Management have been discussed. However there are further opportunities for improving the performance of a Project Supply Chain by applying Operational Excellence concepts. These ideas include Lean, Agile and Six Sigma principles.

With real-time access to the Internet and search engines like Google, as well as increased global competition, customers today have more power than ever before. They demand innovative product features, greater speed, more product variety, dependable performance and quality at a best in class – and at a competitive price. Furthermore, today's discerning consumers expect the fulfilment of their demands almost instantly. The risk attached to the traditional forecast-driven lengthy supply line has become untenable for consumer products. In this chapter we discuss how to take up this challenge through a lean and/or agile supply chain and by using the principles of Six Sigma.

In their 'pure' form three models of supply chain can be identified as being traditional, lean and agile. Let us examine the attributes of each in turn.

Traditional is known for:

- Protection of market, aims for leadership
- Forecast driven
- Higher emphasis on customer service than cost
- Inventory held to buffer fluctuations in demand and lead times.

Lean characteristics are:

- Integration upstream with suppliers
- Integration downstream with customers

- High emphasis on efficiency
- Aims for minimum stock holding.

Agile: noted for flexibility and speed in coping with innovative products and unpredictable demand.

Six Sigma enhances the reliability and dependability of quality by reducing the causes of process variation. If the objective of Six Sigma is the reduction of variation, then Lean aims to accomplish the mission of the organisation better, faster and cheaper. To put it another way, Lean Sigma combines the focus on efficiency by Lean and the emphasis on quality by Six Sigma. There is a trade-off between quality (better), delivery time (faster) and cost (cheaper). Although many supply chains will be a hybrid of these models, it is important to understand the differences and the application of each one, whether pure or hybrid. The traditional supply chain model has been covered in various chapters of this book, so the current section will primarily examine lean and agile models underpinned by Six Sigma. The organisation of this chapter is:

1. The characteristics of a lean supply chain
2. The characteristics of an agile supply chain
3. The strategy of a lean and agile supply chain in major projects
4. Six Sigma in major projects.

THE CHARACTERISTICS OF A LEAN SUPPLY CHAIN

The characteristics and tenets of a Lean Supply Chain are derived from the principles of Toyota Production Systems (TPS) and the methodology of Lean Sigma. Womack and Jones (1998) proposed five lean principles based on Toyota Production Systems, viz. Value, the Value Stream, Flow, Pull and Perfection.

However the application of lean principles has moved with time and according to the experience of organisations in both the manufacturing and service sectors. Until recently supply chains were understood primarily in terms of preparing demand forecasts, upstream collaboration with suppliers and planning and scheduling resources. Emphasis perhaps is shifted to provide what the customers want at a best in class cost. Cost reduction is often the key driver for lean, but it also about speed of delivery and quality of products and service. The competition for gaining and retaining customers and market share is between supply chains rather than other functions of companies. A supply chain therefore has to be lean, with four interrelated key characteristics or objectives:

1. Elimination of waste
2. Smooth operational flow

3. High level of efficiency
4. Quality assurance.

Elimination of Waste

The lean methodology as laid out by Womack and Jones 1998 is sharply focused on the identification and elimination of 'mudas' or waste and their first two principles (i.e. value and value stream) are centred on the elimination of waste. Their motto has been 'banish waste and create wealth in your organisation'. It starts with value stream mapping to identify value and then pinpoint waste with a process mapping of valued processes. The final stage is working systematically to eradicate mudas. This emphasis on waste elimination has probably made lean synonymous with the absence of waste. In fact, waste reduction is often a good place to start in the overall effort to create a lean supply chain because frequently this can be done with little or no capital investment.

One popular area of waste in processes is excess inventory. Many organisations have started to measure their 'leanness' only in terms of inventory performance. Inventory reduction attempts to lessen inventory through such practices as Enterprise Resource Planning (ERP) and Just-In-Time (JIT). Modern approaches to supply chain management have led to lower inventory levels, but there is still plenty of room for improvement. In fact, almost all manufacturers carry at least 25 per cent more inventory than they have to. This inventory-centred approach seems to be encouraged by 'Leanness Studies' (Schonberger, 2003). In these annual reports Schonberger measured the trends in inventory turnover (annual cost of goods divided by value of inventory) and then graded and ranked the companies according to inventory performance. This approach, although a good indicator of the inventory policy of a company, does not necessarily reflect the business performance of that firm. For example the inventory policy of a fast-moving consumer goods (FMCG) business is different from that of a pharmaceutical concern. Inventory constitutes only one of the seven mudas.

Cycle time or lead time reduction is another target area of waste reduction. Cycle time is the period required to complete a given process. The cycle time necessary to proceed a customer order might start with the customer phone call and end with the order being shipped. The overall course of action is made up of many subprocesses, such as order entry, assembly, inspection, packaging and shipping. Cycle Time Reduction lies in identifying and implementing more efficient ways of completing the operation. Reducing cycle time requires eliminating or reducing non-value-added activity. Examples of the types of non-value-added activity in which cycle time can be reduced or eliminated include repair due to defects, machine set-up, inspection, waiting for approval, test and schedule delays.

Smooth Operational Flow

The well-publicised JIT approach is a key driver of the lean supply chain and, as we have indicated earlier, it requires that materials and products flow 'like water' from the supplier through the production process and on to the customer. The capacity bottlenecks are eliminated, the process times of workstations are balanced and there are few buffer inventories between operations. Smooth operational flow requires the application of the most suitable approaches. Two of the most frequently applied methods are:

- Cellular manufacturing
- The Kanban pull system.

Under the cellular manufacturing concept, the traditional batch production area is transformed into flow line layouts so that ideally a single piece runs through the line at any a time. In practice an optimum batch size is calculated, starting with the most critical work centres and the largest inventory carrying costs. Action is taken for improvement at the work centres and methods that have the greatest impact on the throughput, customer satisfaction, operating cost and inventory carrying charges. Good management consists of avoiding a wide variety of products. The cellular manufacturing concept is most appropriate when demand is predictable and products consist of low variety and high volume.

The Toyota Motor Company of Japan pioneered the Kanban technique in the 1980s. As part of the Lean Manufacturing concepts, Kanban was promoted as one of the primary tools of Just-in-Time principles by both Taiichi Ohno (1988) and Shigeo Shingo (1988). Inspired by this technique, American supermarkets in particular replenished shelves as they were emptied, and thus reduced the number of storage spaces, and inventory levels. With a varied degree of success outside Japan, Kanban has been applied to maintain an orderly flow of goods, materials and information throughout the entire operation.

Kanban literally means 'card'. It usually consists of a printed card in a transparent plastic cover that contains specific information regarding part number and quantity. It is a means of pulling parts and products through the manufacturing or logistics sequence as needed. It is therefore sometimes referred to as the 'pull system'. The variants of the Kanban method utilise other markers such as light, electronic signals, voice command or even hand movements.

High Level of Efficiency

The more popular concepts of lean operations tend to be the notions of muda, flow and the pull system. However a preliminary analysis of all these methods, as we have described earlier, highlights the fact that all assume sufficient machine availability exists as a prerequisite. In our experience, for many companies attempting a lean transformation this assumption is just not true. Machine availability depends on maximising the machine up time by eliminating the root causes of down time. The ratio of up time and planned operation time represents the efficiency of the operation. Therefore in order to make lean concepts work it is vital that the precondition of running the operations at a high level of efficiency should be met. The old approach of measuring labour efficiency (e.g. the ratio of standard hours and the time worked) has now shifted to the efficiency of the control or bottleneck workstation.

There are many methodologies and tools for ensuring a high level of competence in a lean supply chain. We are going to describe one such principle (viz. Total Productive Maintenance) and two such tools (Overall Equipment Effectiveness and the 5Ss).

Total productive maintenance (TPM) is a proven Japanese approach to maximising overall equipment effectiveness and utilisation, and relies on attention to detail in all aspects of manufacturing. TPM practices include the operators looking after their own maintenance, and thus encourage empowerment. However the use of the word 'maintenance' in the title is misleading. Total productive maintenance includes more than preservation; rather it addresses all aspects of manufacturing. The two primary goals of TPM are to develop optimum conditions for the factory through a self-help people/machine system culture and to improve the overall quality of the workplace. It involves every employee in the factory. Implementation requires several years, and success relies on sustained management commitment. TPM is promoted throughout the world by the Japan Institute of Plant Maintenance (JIPM).

Quality Assurance

Womack and Jones (1998) propose perfection as the fifth lean principle and according to this a lean manufacturer sets his/her targets for perfection in an incremental (Kaizen) path. The idea of Total Quality Management (TQM) also is to systematically and continuously remove the root causes of poor quality from the production processes so that the organisation as a whole and its products are moving towards perfection. This relentless pursuit of the ideal is a key attitude of an organisation that is 'going for lean'.

The incremental path to total quality management progressively moves from the earlier stages of quality control and quality assurance. Quality assurance focuses on the prevention of failures or defects in a process by analysing the root causes and sustaining the improved process by documenting the standard operating procedure and utilising continuous training. TQM is quality assurance of all processes across the organisation, involving everyone from the top manager to a trainee. Therefore the central driver towards perfection is quality assurance.

This drive for quality assurance has now been extended beyond TQM to Six Sigma, with additional rigour in training deployment (e.g. Black Belts and Green Belts), the methodology of, e.g. Define, Measure, Analyse, Improve and Control (DMAIC) and measurement (both variances and savings). The principles of Six Sigma are embedded in the path towards perfection in a lean supply chain, and Six Sigma has now moved to Lean Sigma and FIT SIGMA. Basu and Wright (2004) explain that the predictable Six Sigma precisions, combined with the speed and agility of Lean, produce definitive solutions for better, faster and cheaper business processes. Through the systematic identification and eradication of non-value-added activities, optimum value flow is achieved, cycle times are reduced and defects eliminated. The dramatic bottom line results and extensive training deployment of Six Sigma and Lean Sigma must be sustained with additional features for securing longer-term competitive advantage.

THE CHARACTERISTICS OF AN AGILE SUPPLY CHAIN

Christopher (2000) defines agility as achieving a rapid response on a global scale to constantly changing markets. This rapid reaction needs to cover changes in demand for both volume and variety. A third dimension concerns lead times and how long it takes to replenish the goods in order to satisfy demand.

Agility is achieved by flexibility and in order to achieve this sort of suppleness, standard platforms are postponed and components and modules are finally assembled when the demand for capacity and variety are known. The standardised elements and modules enable minimum stock keeping of finished products, while at the same time the late assembly makes mass customisation possible with short lead times. Buffer capacity is maintained in order to satisfy the fluctuation of demand. The agile set-up described above demands that the full global supply chain is involved. The subassembly of components into modules can be done in a low-cost environment, whereas the final compilation will often be done close to demand in order to localise the product. Christopher suggests four characteristics of a truly agile supply chain as (1) a market sensitive and capable of reading and responding to real demand; (2) virtual network (e.g. through Internet) which is information based rather than inventory based; (3) process integration ensuring collaborative working between buyers and suppliers; and (4) a network committed to closer and responsive relationships with customers.

Fisher (1997) offers a similar view on the agile and responsive supply chain based on predictable demand versus the unpredictable, but also with the product component of functional versus innovative merchandise. Functional products can be likened to staples that can be bought at groceries and petrol stations. They satisfy basic needs and have a predictable demand with a long life cycle and low profit margin. Innovative products, on the other hand, are like state-of-the-art MP4 players or high fashion clothes. They possess a short life cycle, with higher profit margins but with very unpredictable demand. These distinctions are exemplified as the product life cycle for functional goods is typically more than two years, but for innovative products it can vary from three months to one year. The margin of error for forecasting with functional products is in the 10 per cent range, but for the innovative merchandise it varies from 40 per cent to 100 per cent. Based on the short life cycle and the unpredictable demand and forecasting, it is clear that innovative products need an agile supply chain. This agile supply chain is achieved by buffer capacity and buffer stocks.

Fischer further argues that it is critical that the right supply chain strategy is chosen in order to match the demand and the product, so that innovative goods with a high margin are channelled through a responsive supply chain. The cost of the buffers in capacity and inventory will be offset by a higher margin and a lower number of goods need to be sold. The agile supply chain is achieved, according to Fischer, by adopting four rules, such as (1) accept that uncertainty is inherent in innovative products; (2) reduce that uncertainty by finding data that can support better forecasting; (3) avoid uncertainty by cutting lead times, increasing flexibility in order to produce to order, or move manufacturing closer to demand; and (4) hedge against uncertainty with buffer inventory and excess capacity.

Yusuf et al. (2004) claim that there are four pivotal objectives of agile manufacturing as part of an agile supply chain. These aims are (1) customer enrichment ahead of competitors; (2) achieving mass customisation at the cost of mass production; (3) mastering change and uncertainty through routinely adaptable structures; and (4) leveraging the impact of people across enterprises through information technology. This list clearly shows that enhanced responsiveness is a major capability of an agile supply chain.

In congruence with our research and experience we summarise that in order to achieve the responsiveness required for innovative products, an agile supply chain should contain the following key characteristics:

1. Flexibility
2. Market sensitivity
3. A virtual network
4. Postponement
5. Selected lean supply chain principles.

Flexibility is a key characteristic of an agile supply chain. Flexibility in manufacturing is the ability to respond quickly to the variations of manufacturing requirements in product volume, product variety and of the supply chain. The variability in volume is demonstrated by product launching, seasonal demand, substitution and promotional activities. Changes in variety relate to an increased number of stock keeping units (SKUs) in new products, distributors' own brands (DOB) etc. The variations in the supply chain result from the variability of lead times of both suppliers and customers, increased service levels, change in order size etc. There are instances of failures during the 1980s where companies invested in sophisticated flexible manufacturing systems (FMS) in pursuit of adaptability. At the other end of the scale all the attention was given to organisational flexibility (e.g. cultural and skills integration between craftsmen and operators), producing only limited success. Recognising a closer link between agile processes, there is huge interest in the service sector and also in how to optimise the benefits of agile processes for a faster response to customer demand. In order to improve suppleness in a supply chain it is crucial to reduce complexity in product specifications to maximise mass customisation, lessen complications in processes by standardising them and to enhance organisation flexibility by multiskilling and seamless working practices.

Market sensitivity means that the supply chain is capable of responding to real demand. This requires demand planning not to be driven by periodically adjusted annual forecasts but by actual customer requirements. The scheduling of operations will be reverse timetabling based on customer orders rather than forward planning based on forecast. In addition to actual customer order the use of information technology and both the efficient consumer response (ECR) and customer relationship management (CRM) systems should be utilised to capture data directly from point of sales and consumer buying habits. The growth in 'loyalty cards' and 'store cards' is another source of consumer data to enhance the management of market sensitivity.

'Postponement' is based on the principle that semi-finished products and components are kept in generic form and the ultimate assembly or customisation does not take place until the final customer or market requirements are known. The principle of postponement is an essential characteristic of an agile supply chain. The rapid response tailored to customer needs is also helped by the buffer capacity of key workstations. The point in the supply chain where the semi-finished products are stocked is also known as the 'decoupling' point. This stage should be as close to the market place as possible in the downstream of the supply chain. In addition to responding quickly to specific customer demand, the concept of postponement offers some operational, economic and marketing advantages. As the inventory is kept at a generic level there are fewer SKUs and this makes for easier forecasting and less inventory in total. As the inventory is kept at an earlier stage, thus stock value is also likely to be less than the value of the finished product inventory. A higher level of variety can be offered at a lower cost and marketing can promote apparent exclusivity to customers by 'mass customisation'.

An agile supply chain also shares some lean supply chain principles or characteristics. The enhanced responsiveness of an agile supply chain is in addition to the high level of efficiency, quality assurance and smooth operational flow which are the key characteristics of a lean supply chain. An agile supply chain also focuses on the elimination of waste or mudas as in a lean process, but with a different strategy for buffer capacity and inventory required for postponement. However a pure lean strategy can be applied up to the decoupling point and then an agile method can be utilised beyond that stage. It should be possible to achieve volume-oriented economies of scale up to the decoupling point. This is similar to a service operation (e.g. a bank) where the repetitive activities are isolated or decoupled and carried out in the back office with lean thinking while responsive customer service is provided at the front end.

THE STRATEGY OF A LEAN AND AGILE SUPPLY CHAIN IN MAJOR PROJECTS

The above analysis and our experience strengthen the suitability of a pure agile supply chain for innovative products with an unpredictable demand pattern. In addition, their high profit margin and high variety require many changes and a shorter lead time. A pure lean supply chain, on the other hand, is suitable for high-volume functional products with a lower margin and variety requiring just a few changes. A lean supply chain may also compromise a longer lead time for a lower cost.

A survey by Yusuf et al. (2004), which was carried out by sending a questionnaire to 600 manufacturing companies, showed that only a few firms adopted agile supply chain practices; but many embraced long-term collaboration with suppliers and customers, which was conceptualised as lean supply chain practices. Christopher (2000, p. 37) comments: 'There will be occasions when a pure agile or a lean might be appropriate for a supply chain. However there will often be situations where a combination of the two may be appropriate, i.e. a hybrid strategy.'

In the business world it is more likely that companies have a mixed portfolio of products and services. It is also probable that many high-volume manufacturers or service providers experience short-term or seasonal demand for novelty products (e.g. chocolate eggs at Easter and T-shirts for the Olympics). There will be some high-volume products where demand is stable and more predictable, and there will be products with sporadic demands seeking an agile response. Therefore it is not important to follow either a lean or agile supply chain strategy. However it is vital to recognise that a supply chain can be lean for part of the time, agile for part of the time and both lean and agile (hybrid) for some of the time too.

The initiatives and processes involved in lean project management are deriving benefits from two sources. Firstly, the traditional approach of critical path scheduling (Basu, 2004, p. 129) is to optimise time for completion. Secondly, derived from the lean tools applied in supply chain management (such as value stream and process mapping), the aim is to reduce procurement lead time and non-value-adding activities.

When work on a critical path stops because resources are busy elsewhere or critical supplies are idle, the cause is likely to lie in poor scheduling. The critical path keeps shifting because of the uncertainty of project work. Goldratt (1999), with his 'Critical Chain' and theory of constraints, pointed out that the calculation of 'floats' can be misleading. The apparent buffer of time can evaporate due to preset periods and the allocation of resources. Building on the concept of the 'Critical Chain', lean project management developed and now comprises three major activities:

1. Time buffers are inserted as scheduled amounts of time into projects where non-critical paths feed into the critical path. These act as shock absorbers and keep the critical path stable.
2. Projects are scheduled into the pipeline after checking the availability of resource constraints to ensure that schedules are feasible.
3. Buffer consumption is monitored and tasks feeding into the 'most empty' buffers are given first priority.

Lean project management principles may have provided some good measures to deal with the uncertainty of project work but their apparent complexity is pushing project managers towards the lean approaches of supply chain management. This lean thinking attitude to minimising waste in the project supply chain is championed by the Lean Construction Institute (LCI, www.leanconstruction.org). The goal is to build the project while maximising value, minimising waste and pursuing perfection for the benefit of all project stakeholders. Pinch (2005) explains that the LCI aims are primarily focused on the reduction of waste, as defined by the seven categories of mudas caused by unpredictable workflows. The mudas or wastes identified by Ohno (1973) are:

*   Excess production (no stockpiling of finished goods)
*   Waiting (no buffer stocks between processes, no idle time)
*   Conveyance (reduction of movement to a minimum)
*   Motion (adoption of ergonomic principles)
*   Process (Deming, 1986, claimed that 90 per cent of waste is due to poor processes)
*   Inventory (materials should arrive just as required and flow like water through the system to the end user)
*   Defects (the aim is zero defects – it is cheaper to do things right the first time).

This approach has been defined as lean construction.   By first focusing on workflow, lean construction unplugs clogs in the project stream and gradually planning, design, construction, delivery and closure of the scheme are better coordinated to deliver maximum value for the project owner. Ballard (2001) has proposed a method of reducing cycle time in home-building projects within the context of even flow production. His innovation is the formation of multicraft teams to overlap activities in each phase of the project and also reduce activity durations through time studies.

Case example: lean project management

Morris & Spottiswood is a property solutions business established in 1925 based in Glasgow, Edinburgh and Manchester. The company provides innovative solutions within clients' property space. This is delivered primarily through partnering relationships with leading retail, financial and public sector organisations.

Morris & Spottiswood ran its first Lean project management in 2002/03. The project's scope was to investigate the annual expenditure of externally hired plant. Using techniques such as Pareto Analysis, Value Stream Mapping, Cause and Effect and Implementation Planning, a cross-function team investigated existing processes and established improvements that led to delivery of short, medium and long-term benefits to the business.

The quantifiable savings resulting from the Lean project management was approximately £200,000 in the first year.

Source: Scottish Enterprise, Glasgow (2006); www.scottish-enterprise.com (accessed 7 August 2006)

SIX SIGMA IN MAJOR PROJECTS

Interest in Six Sigma is growing rapidly within the professional project management community, and the most common question coming from that group is something like 'How does Six Sigma relate to the Project Management Body of Knowledge (PMBOK)?' Gack (2006) concludes that Six Sigma and PMBOK do have connections, similarities and distinctions and it is clear that Six Sigma complements and extends professional project management, but does not replace it. Both disciplines make important contributions to successful business outcomes. As described in Chapter 6, the core methodology of Six Sigma – i.e. Define, Measure, Analyse, Improve and

Control (DMAIC) – is closely linked to the methodology, rigour and stages of life cycle of project management.

Even today project managers are not comfortable with embracing Six Sigma in managing their projects, and their arguments include that a project is unique and one off and does not have a stable process and Six Sigma is only effective in repetitive stable processes. They also question whether we need data driven statistics of Six Sigma in projects where contractors are busy just doing their jobs. Our response to these doubts is that Six Sigma can be very effective if the tools and methodology are applied appropriately (fitted to purpose). In *Quality Beyond Six Sigma* (Basu and Wright, 2004) Chapter 8, 'Project Management and FIT SIGMA', addresses the issue of fitness for purpose. In projects we have many repetitive processes and/ or we have many processes requiring design. In both situations DMAIC or Design for Six Sigma (DFSS) can be applied. However the caveat is the appropriateness and for this reason we recommend Six Sigma methodology for larger projects with a longer duration, projects with large management organisations or multinational contractors.

DMAIC has added the rigour of project life cycle to the implementation and close-out of Six Sigma projects. Figure 8.1 shows the relationship between DMAIC and a typical project life cycle.

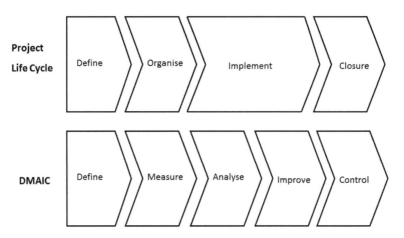

Figure 8.1   DMAIC Life cycle and project life cycle

Project organisations are showing positive interest in Six Sigma, and courses and conferences are on offer for project members. Bechtel was one of the early users of Six Sigma in delivering their multinational projects, as the following case example illustrates.

Case example: Six Sigma at Bechtel

Founded in 1898, Bechtel is one of the world's premier engineering, construction, and project management companies: 40,000 employees are teamed with customers, partners and suppliers on a wide range of projects in nearly 46 countries.

Bechtel has completed more than 22,000 projects in 140 countries, including the Hoover Dam, the Channel Tunnel, Hong Kong International Airport, the reconstruction of Kuwait's oil fields after the Gulf War and Jubail Industrial City.

Bechtel was the first major engineering and construction company to adopt Six Sigma, a data-driven approach to improving efficiency and quality. Although it was originally developed for manufacturing firms, the company was confident that Six Sigma would work in professional services organisations such as Bechtel. Six Sigma has improved every aspect of Bechtel's business, from construction projects to regional offices, saving time and money for both customers and the company.

Six Sigma uses a rigorous set of statistical and analytical tools to produce dramatic improvements in work processes (see Basu and Wright, 2004). Bechtel launched Six Sigma in 2000, when the company was experiencing unprecedented growth – and facing corresponding process challenges. The company has now implemented Six Sigma in its key offices and business units around the world. About half of its employees have had Six Sigma training, and most of its major projects employ its methods from start to finish.

The investment of Bechtel in Six Sigma reached the break-even point in less than three years, and the overall savings have added substantially to the bottom line, while also benefiting customers. Some examples:

- On a big rail modernisation project in the UK, a Bechtel team used Six Sigma to minimise costly train delays caused by project work and reduced the 'break in' period for renovated high-speed tracks.
- At a US Department of Defense site in Maryland, Six Sigma helped achieve significant cost savings by streamlining the analysis of neutralised mustard gas at a project to eliminate chemical weapons.

> - To speed up the location of new cellular sites in big cities, Bechtel developed a way to let planners use computers to view video surveys of streets and buildings, making it easier to pick the best spots.
> - In a mountainous region of Chile, Six Sigma led to more efficient use of equipment in a massive mine expansion, with significant cost savings.
>
> 'Six Sigma is the most important initiative for change we have ever undertaken. We're happy to report that it's becoming "the way we work".'
>
> *Source*: www.bechtel.com (2006)

The introduction of Six Sigma to the High Speed 1 (HS1) project delivered both cost savings and programme benefits. The Six Sigma programme trained 23 Black Belts and around 250 Green Belts and Yellow Belts. A further 100 plus senior managers were educated to act as champions in improvement projects. Over 500 such upgrading schemes were completed, leading to a cost saving/ avoidance of at least £40 million. These ventures covered and benefited a wide range of activities across the whole HS1 task, including numerous architectural, civil and railway construction activities. Consequently this ensured timely third party methodology approvals, thus facilitating procurement, accelerating drawing reviews and allowing the timely generation of construction record documentation. It is evident that some of the improvement projects, such the reduction of lead time in methodology approvals and drawing reviews, also applied Lean Thinking concepts.

SUMMARY

Longer supply chains in major projects with durations spanning several years will mean more dependence on other companies and contractors. Therefore collaboration throughout the project supply chain is becoming a must, as opposed to perpetuating the more traditional adversarial relationships. Indeed, competitive advantage is increasingly arising from the ability to challenge assumptions and deliver projects on time in collaboration with project partners.

In this chapter we demonstrated with case examples how the principles of operational excellence (e.g. Lean, Agile and Six Sigma) can and should be applied in projects – especially major undertakings dealing with several contractors over a number of years – to achieve sustainable, efficient and effective results. The communication and management of stakeholders in a wider community network of a project supply chain still remains a challenge.

We propose that a dedicated supply chain manager should be deployed immediately after the authorisation of major project to manage supply chain activities over the total life cycle of the endeavour. The supply chain manager should assume a function role, similar to a Risk Manager or a Quality Manager, reporting to the Project Director. This role should be to oversee supply chain activities beyond procurement – including supplier partnership, forecasting and scheduling, and other operational excellence initiatives.

Due to the perception of the one-off, unique character of a project and the repetitive nature of operations, the mindsets of many project managers may have a prejudice against or lack the confidence to adopt operational excellence concepts. Leading project contractors such as Bechtel, however, are also training their managers in operational excellence skills (such as those leaders tutored as 'Black Belts'). In a major project or programme with a time span of two years or more, it could be argued that the activities, processes and objectives in the organisation could be closely related to those of operations management. In turn this may well be conducive to the application of operation excellence concepts.

CHAPTER 9

IMPLEMENTATION: MAKING IT HAPPEN

INTRODUCTION

A Supply Chain Manager was recruited from a multinational, fast-moving consumer goods company in a major infrastructure project organisation to implement Supply Chain Management processes in the project. He had gut feeling that his effort was most likely to fail because the Project Manager and the Board viewed supply chain management as a tool for operations management and as a narrow effort in managing projects. The author's experience supports the manager's doubts. The goal of supply chain management is not to produce a silver bullet to solve all procurement and supply problems. It is indeed a holistic process involving all key members of the project team, suppliers and contractors. The aim of this chapter is to outline how the key deliverables from previous chapters can be pulled together to benefit from managing an integrated supply project supply chain and highlight the critical success factors of making it happen.

A HOLISTIC APPROACH

It is fundamental to project success that materials, supplies and equipment are delivered on time, cost and quality. The previous chapters have demonstrated that supply chain management building blocks and methods are key to ensuring that project resources arrive as required. In order to make it happen we need a holistic approach to build an integrated project supply chain with the building blocks (see Chapters 3 and 4) and integrating processes (see Chapters 5, 6 and 7).

Chapter 1 provides an overview of supply chain management principles. It aimed to indicate how an effective supply chain management process adds value to all types of businesses, whether in the manufacturing or service sectors, public or not-for-profit organisations. It is also emphasised that in a project supply chain a major contractor is served by several subcontractors and each subcontractor may be served by several other subcontractors and the process becomes more complex. It is critical to have data sharing and interaction between all stakeholders in the Total Supply Chain.

The concept of the total supply chain is expanded in Chapter 2. The building blocks consist of nine components, out of which six are for supply chain configuration and three components are for supply chain integration. It is important to recognise the tangible deliverables and interdependence of each building block to apply a total supply chain approach to achieve project success.

In Chapter 3 we have explained the role and importance of the three building blocks in the project planning chain. The criticality of defining the project scope and proportionately engaging stakeholders is very well established in project management principles. In the integration of a project supply chain the role of the supply chain manager should be established during the development of the business case and the planning of resources and time management. The supply chain manager can act as inculcating the culture of integration of stakeholders with the total supply chain. Procurement and supplier focus is arguably the most vital building block of a project supply chain, where both the ownership and leadership of the supply chain manager is most evident. In managing the top tier suppliers and contract there are likely to be two categories. The high-risk contracts should be managed with minimum changes and well-defined responsibilities of suppliers. The medium- and low-risk contracts should be managed as non-adversary supplier partnerships.

The building blocks and process of the delivery supply chain is discussed in Chapter 4. The author's experience suggests that this post-contract phase of the project is often left to major contractors and the role of the supply chain manager is sidelined. There is a considerable risk is reducing the focus of supply chain management during the building and handover activities. The critical factors include the forecasting of demand, stock management and logistics support to ensure that resources and materials are available on time, and the close-out of all purchase orders.

Although the integration processes of the project supply chain have been discussed in Chapters 5, 6 and 7 it is emphasised that these processes are the glues that bind the stakeholders and tangible deliverables of other building blocks and make things happen as a holistic process. The procurement process is closely guided by NEC3 (2005) and the general governance of project supply chains is also guided by PMBOK (2008) and PRINCE2 (2009) as appropriate. As discussed in Chapter 5, project management software (e.g. MS Project and Oracle Primavera) are useful tools to control procurement schedules and to bring together the business collaboration services. We have shown in Chapter 6 that project quality has three dimensions – design quality, process quality and organisation quality. A good quality management system in managing project supply chains should be underpinned by a properly designed Balanced Scorecard based performance management system, as the experience of the T5 project demonstrated. The importance of regular reviews by progressive meetings has been explained and emphasised in Chapter 7. Even if good systems and processes are in place the involvement and appropriate commitments of all members and key stakeholders of the project are essential for its success.

The success of a project, and for that matter the management of project supply chains, is realised over time when the outcomes delivered by the project are sustained to the satisfaction of stakeholders. This leads to project excellence assisted by operational excellence concepts. It is also important that project supply chains should be lean and agile. In Chapter 8 we demonstrated with case examples how the principles of Operational Excellence (e.g. Lean, Agile and Six Sigma) can and should be applied in projects – especially major undertakings dealing with several contractors over a number of years – to achieve sustainable, efficient and effective results.

SUCCESS FACTORS

On a closer examination, it is apparent that success criteria and success factors are closely linked to the dimensions of project quality. Many success criteria of Grude et al. (1996) (such as 'meets user requirements', 'achieves purpose') appear to relate closely to Turner's (2007) 'product quality'. Some of the 'hard' success factors, especially of Pinto and Slevin (1988) (such as 'monitoring and feedback') also relate to Turner's 'process quality'.

It is important to note that although different authors identified various lists of success factors, the common theme and most of the 'soft' or people-related factors of Pinto and Slevin –such as 'top management support', 'client consultation', 'communication', 'personnel' – appear to be closely related to the factors governing the 'organisation quality' as defined by Basu (2004). The four conditions of project success as given by Jugdev and Muller (2005) also reflect the importance of people-related 'organisation quality'.

By extending the theme of organisation quality to project supply chains it is argued that critical success factors of managing supply chains in projects would include many people-related enablers. There are also specific action points contributing to the success outcomes of managing project chains to deliver project resources on time, quality and cost to the satisfaction of key stakeholders.

The critical project success factors should include:

1. Clear objectives
2. Top management commitment
3. Appropriate skills and organisation
4. Clearly assigned responsibility, with clear reporting structure
5. Support of all stakeholders
6. Early planning is most important, with definite start

7. Using the right tools for planning and control
8. Managing risk
9. Allowing enough time and money (hold contingency)
10. One good project leader
11. Careful communication and monitoring
12. Lessons learnt from past experience and continuous training.

The specific action points related to successfully managing a project supply chain should include:

1. Appoint a supply chain manager during the development of the business case with the full support of the Project Board.
2. Engage stakeholders, proportionate to their interest and influence, with a structured engagement plan and schedule.
3. Enhance among key stakeholders a clear understanding of the role and interrelationship of the supply chain building blocks.
4. Develop a procurement strategy according to the expertise and capacity of the in-house project team.
5. Follow a structured process of selecting major contractors to obtain value for money and service.
6. Identify high-risk contracts with minimum changes and legally binding service agreements and develop supplier partnerships for medium- and low-risk contracts.
7. Ensure stock management and logistic support during the construction and handover stages of the project until the closure of each purchase order.
8. Recruit, train and motivate the right people to manage supply chain processes in harmony with key stakeholders.
9. Ensure the integrating processes of managing supply chains (e.g. systems and procedures, quality systems and regular reviews) are in place.
10. Apply operational excellence concepts in managing supply chains to achieve longer-term benefits of project excellence.

CONCLUDING REMARKS

The theme, focus and scope of the book are more appropriate for managing supply chains in major projects. In this book the author has also aimed to present supply chain management as an interface between operations and projects and this interface and and some operational concepts (e.g. Six Sigma) work well when a major project is managed as an enterprise. However the concepts, building blocks and processes presented in this book should also benefit smaller projects with multiple suppliers and complex requirements of resources.

REFERENCES

Ala-Risku, T. and Karkkainen, M. (2006), 'Material delivery problems in construction: a possible solution', *International Journal of Production Economics*, Volume 104, No. 1, pp. 19–29.

Association for Project Management (APM) (2006), *The Body of Knowledge*, APM, High Wycombe; www.apm.org.uk.

Atkinson, R. (1999), 'Project management: cost, time and quality, two best guesses and a phenomenon, its time to accept other success criteria', *International Journal of Project Management*, Volume 17, No. 6, pp. 337–42.

Ballard, G. (2001), 'Cycle Time Reduction in Home Building', Proceedings of the 9th Annual Conference of the International Group for Lean Construction, Singapore, August 2001.

Barlow, R.D. (2010), 'Kept in the dark', *Healthcare Purchasing News*, February, pp. 48–9.

Barsodi, R (1929), *The Distribution Age*, Appleton and Co., New York.

Basu, R. (2002), *Measuring e-Business in the Pharmaceutical Sector*, Business Insight Report, Reuters, London.

Basu, R (2004), 'Six-Sigma to operational excellence: role of tools and techniques', *International Journal of Six Sigma and Competitive Advantage*, Volume 1, No. 1, pp. 44–64.

Basu, R. (2009), *Implementing Six Sigma and Lean*, Elsevier, Oxford.

Basu, R. (2010), 'In search of project excellence', *International Journal of Business and Systems Research*, Volume 4, No. 4, pp. 432–50.

Basu, R. (2011), *FIT SIGMA*, John Wiley and sons, Chichester.

Basu, R. and Wright, J.N. (2004), *Quality Beyond Six Sigma*, Elsevier, Oxford.

Basu, R. and Wright, J.N. (2005), *Total Operations Solutions*, Butterworth Heinemann, Oxford.

Basu, R. and Wright, J.N. (2008), *Total Supply Chain Management*, Elsevier, Oxford.

Basu, R., Little, C. and Millard, C. (2009), 'Case study: a fresh approach of the Balanced Scorecard in the Heathrow Terminal 5 project', *Measuring Business Excellence*, Volume 13, No. 4, pp. 22–33.

Best Practices LLC (2000), *Building Six Sigma Excellence: A Case Study of General Electric*, Best Practices LLC, www.best-in-class.cpm.

British Standard Institute (2002), *BS 6079: A Guide to Project Management*, BSI, London.

Cap Gemini (2005), *Trends in Project Performance Improvement*, Capgemini Netherlands, Utrecht.

Christopher, M. (1992), *Logistics and Supply Chain Management*, Pitman, London

Christopher, M. (2000), 'The agile supply chain', *Industrial Marketing Management*, Volume 29, No. 1, pp. 37–44.

Deming, W.E. (1986), *Out of the Crisis*, MIT Centre for Advanced Research, Cambridge, MA.

Easton, G.S. and Jarrell, S.L. (1998), 'The effects of total quality management on corporate performance: an empirical investigation', *Journal of Business*, Volume 71, No. 2, pp. 253–307.

Feigenbaum, A.V. (1983), *Total Quality Control*, McGraw-Hill, New York.

Fisher, M.L. (1997), 'What is the right supply chain for your product?', *Harvard Business Review*, March–April, pp. 105–16.

Gack, G. (2006), 'How does Six Sigma relate to the Project Management Body of Knowledge (PMBoK)?', http://software.isixsigma.com (accessed 7 August 2006).

Garvin, D. (1984), 'What does "product quality" really mean?', *Sloan Management Review*, Volume 26, No. 1, pp. 25–43.

Goldratt, E.M. (1999), *The Theory of Constraints*, North River Press, Great Barrington, MA.

Grude, K., Turner, R. and Wateridge, J. (1996), 'Project Health Checks', in Turner, R., Grude, K. and Thurloway, L. (eds), *The Project Manager as Change Agent*, McGraw-Hill, London.

Hamilton, A. (2004), *Handbook of Project Management Procedures*, Thomas Telford, London.

Heisler, S.I. (1990), 'Project quality and the project manager', *International Journal of Project Management*, Volume 8, No. 3, pp. 133–7.

Herman, D.R. and Renz, D.O. (2002), 'Advancing nonprofit organizational effectiveness research and theory: nine theses', *Nonprofit Management and Leadership*, Volume 18, No. 4, pp. 339–415.

International Standard Organisation (2003), *ISO 10006: Quality Management Systems – Guidelines for Quality Management in Projects*, ISO, Geneva.

Jugdev, K and Muller, R. (2005), 'Process success: a retrospective look at project success and our evolving understanding of concept', *Project Management Journal*, Volume 36, No. 4, pp. 19–31.

Juran, J.M. (1989), *Juran on Leadership for Quality: An Executive Handbook*, Free Press, New York.

Kaplan, R.S. and Norton, D.P. (1996), *Balanced Scorecard*, Harvard Business School Press, Boston, MA.

Kaplan, R.S. and Norton, D.P. (2004), 'Measuring the strategic readiness of intangible assets', *Harvard Business Review*, Volume 82, No. 2, pp. 52–64.

Keegan, A., Turner, R. and Huemann, M. (2008), 'Managing Human Resources in the Project Based Organization', in Turner, J.R. (ed.), *Gower Handbook of Project Management*, Gower Publishing, Aldershot, 4th edition.

Kotnour, T. (2000), 'Organisational learning practices in the project management environment', *The International Journal of Quality and Reliability Management*, Volume 17, No. 4/5, pp. 393–406.

Levitt, J.S. and Nann, P.C. (1994), *Total Quality Through Project Management*, McGraw-Hill, New York.

Ling, R.C. and Goddard, W.E. (1988), *Orchestrating Success: Improve Control of the Business with Sales and Operations Planning*, J. Wiley & Sons, Christchurch.

McElroy, B. and Mills, C. (2000), 'Managing Stakeholders', in Turner, J. and Simister, S. (eds), *Gower Handbook of Project Management*, Gower Publishing, Aldershot.

McKenna, M. and Wilczynski, H. (2005), *Capital is Real Money Too*, Booz Allen Hamilton Inc, USA.

Meredith, J.R. and Mantel, S.J. (2003), *Project Management: A Managerial Approach*, J. Wiley & Sons, New York.

Mitchell, V.W. (1998), 'Buy-phase and buy-class effects on organisational risk perception and reduction in purchasing professional services', *The Journal of Business & Industrial Marketing*, Volume 13, No. 6, pp. 461–71.

Morris, P.W.G. (1973), 'Organizational analysis of project management in the building industry', *Build International*, Vol. 6, No. 6, pp. 595–616.

Morris, P.W.G. (1997), *The Management of Projects*, Thomas Telford, London.

National Audit Office (NAO) (2000), *The Millennium Dome*, NAO, London.

NEC3 (2005), *Procurement and Contract Strategies*, Office of Government Commerce, London.

Nichols, M. and Jones, S. (2010), 'The Genesis of Project Personality', Major Projects Association 28th Annual Conference, Chesham, Bucks, 23–4 September 2010.

O'Brien, W. (2001), 'Enabling Technologies for Project Supply Chain Collaboration', NSF/ICIS Infrastructure and Information Technology Workshop, Arlington, VA, June 2001.

Oakland, J.S. (2003), *TQM: Text with Cases*, Butterworth Heinemann, Oxford.

Ohno, T. (1988), *The Toyota Production System: Beyond Large-Scale Production*, Productivity Press, Cambridge, MA.

Parasuraman, A., Zeithamel, V. and Berry, L. (1984), 'A conceptual model of service quality', *Journal of Marketing*, Volume 49, No. 3, pp. 41–50.

Pharro, R. (2002), 'Processes and Procedures', in Turner, R. and Simister, S. (eds), *Gower Handbook of Project Management*, Gower Publishing, Aldershot, 3rd edition.

Pinch, L. (2005), 'Lean construction', *Construction Executive*, Volume 15, No. 11, pp. 8–11.

Pinto, J.K. and Slevin, D.P. (1988), 'Critical Success Factors in Effective Project Implementation', in Cleland, D.J. and King, W.R. (eds), *Project Management Handbook*, Van Nostrand Reinhold, New York.

Porter, M.E. (1985), *Competitive Strategy*, Free Press, New York.

PRINCE2 (2009), *Understanding PRINCE2*, SPOCE, Bournemouth.

Project Management Institute (PMI) (2008), *A Guide to the Project Management Body of Knowledge (PMBOK® Guide)*, PMI, Newtown Square, PA.

Reid, R.D. and Sanders, N.R. (2002), *Operation Management*, J. Wiley & Sons, Chichester.

Saaty, T.L. (1996), *Analytical Network Process*, RWS Publications, Pittsburgh.

Schonberger, R. (2003), *World Class Manufacturing*, Free Press, New York.

Shingo, S. (1988), *A Revolution in Manufacturing: The SMED System*, Productivity Press, Cambridge, MA.

Simchi-Levi, D., Kaminsky, P. and Simchi-Levi, E. (2003), *Designing and Managing the Supply Chain*, McGraw-Hill, London, 2nd edition.

Slack, N., Chambers, S., Johnston, R. and Betts, A. (2006), *Operations and Process Management*, FT Prentice Hall, London.

Smith, N. (2000), 'Roles and Responsibilities in Project Procurement', in Turner, R. and Simister, S. (eds), *Gower Handbook of Project Management*, Gower Publishing, Aldershot, 3rd edition.

Sterman, J.D., Keating, E.K., Oliva, R, Repenning, N.P. and Rockart, S. (1999), 'Overcoming the improvement paradox', *European Management Journal*, Volume 17, No. 2, pp. 120–34.

Swank, C.K. (2003), 'The lean service machine', *Harvard Business Review*, Volume 81, No. 10, pp. 123–9.

Swink, M., Melnyk, M., Cooper, B. and Hartley, J. (2010), *Managing Operations Across the Supply Chain*, McGraw-Hill, Maidenhead.

Tabassi, A.K. and Bakar, A.H. (2009), 'Training, motivation and performance; the case of human resource management in construction projects', *International Journal of Project Management*, Volume 27, No. 5, pp. 471–80.

Taylor, D. (1997), *Global Cases in Logistics and Supply Chain Management*, Thomson Learning, London.

Transport Select Committee (2008), 'Transport Twelfth Report', Louise Ellman MP (Chair), House of Commons Publications, London, printed 22 October 2008.

Tuckman, B. (1965), 'Developing sequence in small groups', *Psychological Bulletin*, Volume 63, No. 6, pp. 384–99.

Turner, R. (1999), *The Handbook of Project Based Management*, McGraw-Hill, London

Turner, R. (2007), 'Managing Quality', in Turner, R. (ed.), *Gower Handbook of Project Management*, Gower Publishing, Aldershot, 4th edition.

Wade, R. (2003), 'What strategies are viable for developing countries today? The World Trade Organization and the shrinking of "development space"', *Review of International Political Economy*, Volume 10, No. 4. pp. 621–44.

Waller, M. (2005), 'Hurricane Katrina showed importance of logistics and supply chain management', *Supply & Demand Chain Executive*, 10 October 2005.

Wateridge, J (2002), 'Project Health Checks', in Turner, R. and Simister, S. (eds), *Gower Handbook of Project Management*, Gower Publishing, Aldershot, 3rd edition.

Weinstein, L.B., Castellano, J., Petrick, J. and Vokurka, R.J. (2008), 'Integrating Six Sigma concepts in an MBA quality management class', *Journal of Education for Business*, Volume 83, No. 4, pp. 233–8.

Westerveld, E. (2003),'The project excellence model', *International Journal of Project Management*, Volume 21, No. 6, pp. 411–18.

Wild, R. (2002), *Essentials of Operations Management*, Thomson Learning, London.

Womack, J. and Jones, D, (1998), *Lean Thinking*, Touchstone Books, London.

Womack, J., Jones, D. and Roos, D. (1990), *The Machine That Changed The World*, Rawson and Associates, New York.

Yusuf, Y.Y., Gunasekaran, A., Adeleye, E.O. and Sivayoganathan, K (2004), 'Agile supply chain capabilities: determinants of competitive objectives', *European Journal of Operational Research*, Volume 159, No. 2, pp. 379–92.

INDEX

ADVANCES IN PROJECT MANAGEMENT

Advances in Project Management provides short, state of play guides to the main aspects of the new emerging applications, including: maturity models, agile projects, extreme projects, Six Sigma and projects, human factors and leadership in projects, project governance, value management, virtual teams and project benefits.

Currently Published Titles

Managing Project Uncertainty, David Cleden 978-0-566-08840-7

Project-Oriented Leadership, Ralf Müller and J. Rodney Turner 978-0-566-08923-7

Second Order Project Management, Michael Cavanagh 978-1-4094-1094-2

Strategic Project Risk Appraisal and Management, Elaine Harris 978-0-566-08848-3

Sustainability in Project Management, Gilbert Silvius, Jasper van den Brink, Ron Schipper, Adri Köhler and Julia Planko 978-1-4094-3169-5

Tame, Messy and Wicked Risk Leadership, David Hancock 978-0-566-09242-8

Reviews of the Series

Managing Project Uncertainty, David Cleden

> *This is a must-read book for anyone involved in project management. The author's carefully crafted work meets all my "4Cs" review criteria. The book is clear, cogent, concise and complete ... it is a brave author who essays to write about managing project uncertainty in a text extending to only 117 pages (soft-cover version). In my opinion, David Cleden succeeds brilliantly. ... For*

project managers this book, far from being a short-lived stress anodyne, will provide a confidence-boosting tonic. Project uncertainty? Bring it on, I say!
International Journal of Managing Projects in Business

Uncertainty is an inevitable aspect of most projects, but even the most proficient project manager struggles to successfully contain it. Many projects overrun and consume more funds than were originally budgeted, often leading to unplanned expense and outright programme failure. David examines how uncertainty occurs and provides management strategies that the user can put to immediate use on their own project work. He also provides a series of pre-emptive uncertainty and risk avoidance strategies that should be the cornerstone of any planning exercise for all personnel involved in project work.
I have been delivering both large and small projects and programmes in the public and private sector since 1989. I wish this book had been available when I began my career in project work. I strongly commend this book to all project professionals.
Lee Hendricks, Sales & Marketing Director, SunGard Public Sector

The book under review is an excellent presentation of a comprehensive set of explorations about uncertainty (its recognition) in the context of projects. It does a good job of all along reinforcing the difference between risk (known unknowns) management and managing uncertainty (unknown unknowns – "bolt from the blue"). The author lucidly presents a variety of frameworks/ models so that the reader easily grasps the varied forms in which uncertainty presents itself in the context of projects.
VISION: The Journal of Business Perspective (India)

Cleden will leave you with a sound understanding about the traits, tendencies, timing and tenacity of uncertainty in projects. He is also adept at identifying certain methods that try to contain the uncertainty, and why some prove more successful than others. Those who expect risk management to be the be-all, end-all for uncertainty solutions will be in for a rude awakening.
Brad Egeland, Project Management Tips

Strategic Project Risk Appraisal and Management, Elaine Harris

Elaine Harris's volume is timely. In a world of books by "instant experts" it's pleasing to read something by someone who clearly knows their onions, and has a passion for the subject. In summary, this is a thorough and engaging book.
Chris Morgan, Head of Business Assurance for Select Plant Hire,
Quality World

As soon as I met Elaine I realised that we both shared a passion to better understand the inherent risk in any project, be that capital investment, expansion capital or expansion of assets. What is seldom analysed are the components of knowledge necessary to make a good judgement, the impact of our own prejudices in relation to projects or for that matter the cultural elements within an organisation which impact upon the decision making process. Elaine created a system to break this down and give reasons and logic to both the process and the human interaction necessary to improve the chances of success. Adopting her recommendations will improve teamwork and outcomes for your company.

Edward Roderick Hon. LLD, former CEO Christian Salvesen plc

Tame, Messy and Wicked Risk Leadership, David Hancock

This book takes project risk management firmly onto a higher and wider plane. We thought we knew what project risk management was and what it could do. David Hancock shows us a great deal more of both. David Hancock has probably read more about risk management than almost anybody else; he has almost certainly thought about it as much as anybody else and he has quite certainly learnt from doing it on very difficult projects as much as anybody else. His book draws fully on all three components. For a book which tackles a complex subject with breadth, insight and novelty – it's remarkable that it is also a really good read. I could go on!

Dr Martin Barnes CBE FREng, President, The Association for
Project Management

This compact and thought-provoking description of risk management will be useful to anybody with responsibilities for projects, programmes or businesses. It hits the nail on the head in so many ways, for example by pointing out that risk management can easily drift into a checklist mindset, driven by the production of registers of numerous occurrences characterised by the Risk = Probablity × Consequence equation. David Hancock points out that real life is much more complicated, with the heart of the problem lying in people, so that real life resembles poker rather than roulette. He also points out that while the important thing is to solve the right problem, many real-life issues cannot be readily described in a definitive statement of the problem. There are often interrelated individual problems with surrounding social issues and he describes these real-life situations as "Wicked Messes". Unusual terminology, but definitely worth the read, as much for the overall problem description as for the recommended strategies for getting to grips with real-life risk management. I have no hesitation in recommending this book.

Sir Robert Walmsley KCB FREng, Chairman of the Board of the Major
Projects Association

*In highlighting the complexity of many of today's problems and defining them
as tame, messy or wicked, David Hancock brings a new perspective to the risk
issues that we currently face. He challenges risk managers, and particularly
those involved in project risk management, to take a much broader approach
to the assessment of risk and consider the social, political and behavioural
dimensions of each problem, as well as the scientific and engineering aspects
with which they are most comfortable. In this way, risks will be viewed more
holistically and managed more effectively than at present.*

Dr Lynn T. Drennan, Chief Executive Alarm, The Public Risk
Management Association

About the Editor

Professor Darren Dalcher is founder and Director of the National Centre for
Project Management, a Professor of Software Project Management at Middlesex
University and Visiting Professor of Computer Science at the University of Iceland.
Professor Dalcher has been named by the Association for Project Management as
one of the top 10 'movers and shapers' in project management. He has also been
voted *Project Magazine*'s Academic of the Year for his contribution in 'integrating
and weaving academic work with practice'.

Professor Dalcher is active in numerous international committees, steering groups
and editorial boards. He is heavily involved in organising international conferences,
and has delivered many keynote addresses and tutorials. He has written over 150
papers and book chapters on project management and software engineering. He is
Editor-in-Chief of *Software Process Improvement and Practice*, an international
journal focusing on capability, maturity, growth and improvement.

Professor Dalcher is a Fellow of the Association for Project Management and the
British Computer Society, and a Member of the Project Management Institute, the
Academy of Management, the Institute for Electrical and Electronics Engineers and
the Association for Computing Machinery. He is a Chartered IT Practitioner. He is a
member of the PMI Advisory Board responsible for the prestigious David I. Cleland
project management award, and of the APM Professional Development Board.

National Centre for Project Management
Middlesex University
College House
Trent Park
Bramley Road
London N14 4YZ
Email: ncpm@mdx.ac.uk
Phone: +44 (0)20 8411 2299